Oracle SQL Tuning
Pocket Reference

Oracle SQL Tuning
Pocket Reference

Mark Gurry

Beijing · Cambridge · Farnham · Köln · Paris · Sebastopol · Taipei · Tokyo

Oracle SQL Tuning Pocket Reference
by Mark Gurry

Copyright © 2002 O'Reilly & Associates, Inc. All rights reserved.
Printed in the United States of America.

Published by O'Reilly & Associates, Inc., 1005 Gravenstein Highway
North, Sebastopol, CA 95472.

Editor:	Jonathan Gennick
Production Editor:	Jane Ellin
Cover Designer:	Ellie Volckhausen
Interior Designer:	David Futato

Printing History:

January 2002: First Edition.

0-596-00268-8
[C]

Contents

Oracle SQL Tuning
Pocket Reference

Introduction

This book is a quick-reference guide for tuning Oracle SQL. This is not a comprehensive Oracle tuning book.

The purpose of this book is to give you some light reading material on my "real world" tuning experiences and those of my company, Mark Gurry & Associates. We tune many large Oracle sites. Many of those sites, such as banks, large financial institutions, stock exchanges, and electricity markets, are incredibly sensitive to poor performance.

With more and more emphasis being placed on 24/7 operation, the pressure to make SQL perform in production becomes even more critical. When a new SQL statement is introduced, we have to be absolutely sure that it is going to perform. When a new index is added, we have to be certain that it will not be used inappropriately by existing SQL statements. This book addresses these issues.

Many sites are now utilizing third-party packages such as Peoplesoft, SAP, Oracle Applications, Siebel, Keystone, and others. Tuning SQL for these applications must be done without placing hints on SQL statements, because you are unauthorized to touch the application code. Obviously, for similar reasons, you can't rewrite the SQL. But don't lose heart; there are many tips and tricks in this reference that will assist you when tuning packaged software.

This book portrays the message, and my firm belief, that there is always a way of improving your performance to make it acceptable to your users.

Acknowledgments

Many thanks to my editor, Jonathan Gennick. His feedback and suggestions have added significant improvements and clarity to this book. A hearty thanks to my team of technical reviewers: Sanjay Mishra, Stephen Andert, and Tim Gorman. Thanks also to my Mark Gurry & Associates consultants for their technical feedback. Special thanks to my wife Juliana for tolerating me during yet another book writing exercise.

Caveats

This book does not cover every type of environment, nor does it cover all performance tuning scenarios that you will encounter as an Oracle DBA or developer.

I can't stress enough the importance of regular hands-on testing in preparation for being able to implement your performance tuning recommendations.

Conventions

UPPERCASE
    Indicates a SQL keyword

lowercase
    Indicates user-defined items such as tablespace names and datafile names

Constant width
    Used for examples showing code

Constant width bold
    Used for emphasis in code examples

[]
    Used in syntax descriptions to denote optional elements

{}

    Used in syntax descriptions to denote a required choice

|

    Used in syntax descriptions to separate choices

What's New in Oracle9i

It's always exciting to get a new release of Oracle. This section briefly lists the new Oracle9i features that will assist us in getting SQL performance to improve even further than before. The new features are as follows:

- A new INIT.ORA parameter, FIRST_ROWS_n, that allows the cost-based optimizer to make even better informed decisions on the optimal execution path for an OLTP application. The *n* can equal 1, 10, 100, or 1,000. If you set the parameter to FIRST_ROWS_1, Oracle will determine the optimum execution path to return one row; FIRST_ROWS_10 will be the optimum plan to return ten rows; and so on.

- There is a new option called SIMILAR for use with the CURSOR_SHARING parameter. The advantages of sharing cursors include reduced memory usage, faster parses, and reduced latch contention. SIMILAR changes literals to bind variables, and differs from the FORCE option in that similar statements can share the same SQL area without resulting in degraded execution plans.

- There is a new hint called CURSOR_SHARING_EXACT that allows you to share cursors for all statements except those with this hint. In essence, this hint turns off cursor sharing for an individual statement.

- There is a huge improvement in overcoming the skewness problem. The skewness problem comes about because a bind variable is evaluated after the execution plan is decided. If you have 1,000,000 rows with STATUS = 'C' for Closed, and 100 rows with STATUS = 'O' for Open, Oracle should use the index on STATUS when you query for STATUS = 'O', and should perform a full table scan when you query for STATUS = 'C'. If you used bind variables prior to Oracle9*i*, Oracle would assume a 50/50 spread for both values, and would use a full table scan in either case. Oracle 9*i* determines the value of the bind variable *prior to* deciding on the execution plan. Problem solved!

- You can now identify unused indexes using the ALTER INDEX MONITOR USAGE command.

- You can now use DBMS_STATS to gather SYSTEM statistics, including a system's CPU and I/O usage. You may find that disks are a bottleneck, and Oracle will then have the information to adjust the execution plans accordingly.

- There are new hints, including NL_AJ, NL_SJ, FACT, NO_FACT, and FIRST_ROWS(n). All are described in detail in the "Using SQL Hints" section of this reference.

- Outlines were introduced with Oracle8*i* to allow you to force execution plans (referred to as "outlines") for selected SQL statements. However, it was sometimes tricky to force a SQL statement to use a particular execution path. Oracle9*i* provides us with the ultimate: we can now edit the outline using the DBMS_OUTLN_EDIT package.

The SQL Optimizers

Whenever you execute a SQL statement, a component of the database known as the *optimizer* must decide how best to access the data operated on by that statement. Oracle supports two optimizers: the rule-base optimizer (which was the original), and the cost-based optimizer.

To figure out the optimal execution path for a statement, the optimizers consider the following:

- The syntax you've specified for the statement
- Any conditions that the data must satisfy (the WHERE clauses)

- The database tables your statement will need to access
- All possible indexes that can be used in retrieving data from the table
- The Oracle RDBMS version
- The current optimizer mode
- SQL statement hints
- All available object statistics (generated via the ANALYZE command)
- The physical table location (distributed SQL)
- INIT.ORA settings (parallel query, async I/O, etc.)

Oracle gives you a choice of two optimizing alternatives: the predictable rule-based optimizer and the more intelligent cost-based optimizer.

Understanding the Rule-Based Optimizer

The rule-based optimizer (RBO) uses a predefined set of precedence rules to figure out which path it will use to access the database. The RDBMS kernel defaults to the rule-based optimizer under a number of conditions, including:

- OPTIMIZER_MODE = RULE is specified in your INIT.ORA file
- OPTIMIZER_MODE = CHOOSE is specified in your INIT.ORA file, and no statistics exist for *any* table involved in the statement
- An ALTER SESSION SET OPTIMIZER_MODE = RULE command has been issued
- An ALTER SESSION SET OPTIMIZER_MODE = CHOOSE command has been issued, and no statistics exist for *any* table involved in the statement
- The rule hint (e.g., SELECT /*+ RULE */. . .) has been used in the statement

The rule-based optimizer is driven primarily by 20 condition rankings, or "golden rules." These rules instruct the optimizer how to determine the execution path for a statement, when to choose one index over another, and when to perform a full table scan. These rules, shown in Table 1, are fixed, predetermined, and, in contrast with the cost-based optimizer, not influenced by outside sources (table volumes, index distributions, etc.).

Table 1. Rule-based optimizer condition rankings

Rank	Condition
1	ROWID = constant
2	Cluster join with unique or primary key = constant
3	Hash cluster key with unique or primary key = constant
4	Entire Unique concatenated index = constant
5	Unique indexed column = constant
6	Entire cluster key = corresponding cluster key of another table in the same cluster
7	Hash cluster key = constant
8	Entire cluster key = constant
9	Entire non-UNIQUE CONCATENATED index = constant
10	Non-UNIQUE index merge
11	Entire concatenated index = lower bound
12	Most leading column(s) of concatenated index = constant
13	Indexed column between low value and high value or indexed column LIKE "ABC%" (bounded range)
14	Non-UNIQUE indexed column between low value and high value or indexed column like 'ABC%' (bounded range)
15	UNIQUE indexed column or constant (unbounded range)
16	Non-UNIQUE indexed column or constant (unbounded range)
17	Equality on non-indexed = column or constant (sort/merge join)
18	MAX or MIN of single indexed columns
19	ORDER BY entire index
20	Full table scans

While knowing the rules is helpful, they alone do not tell you enough about how to tune for the rule-based optimizer. To overcome this deficiency, the following sections provide some information that the rules don't tell you.

What the RBO rules don't tell you #1

Only single column indexes are ever merged. Consider the following SQL and indexes:

```
SELECT col1, ...
  FROM emp
 WHERE emp_name = 'GURRY'
   AND emp_no   = 127
   AND dept_no  = 12

Index1 (dept_no)
Index2 (emp_no, emp_name)
```

The SELECT statement looks at all three indexed columns. Many people believe that Oracle will merge the two indexes, which involve those three columns, to return the requested data. In fact, only the two-column index is used; the single-column index is not used. While Oracle *will* merge two single-column indexes, it *will not* merge a multi-column index with another index.

There is one thing to be aware of with respect to this scenario. If the single-column index is a unique or primary key index, that would cause the single-column index to take precedence over the multi-column index. Compare rank 4 with rank 9 in Table 1.

NOTE

Oracle8*i* introduced a new hint, INDEX_JOIN, that allows you to join multi-column indexes.

What the RBO rules don't tell you #2

If all columns in an index are specified in the WHERE clause, that index will be used in preference to other indexes for which *some* columns are referenced. For example:

```
SELECT col1, ...
  FROM emp
 WHERE emp_name = 'GURRY'
   AND emp_no   = 127
   AND dept_no  = 12

Index1 (emp_name)
Index2 (emp_no, dept_no, cost_center)
```

In this example, only Index1 is used, because the WHERE clause includes all columns for that index, but does not include all columns for Index2.

What the RBO rules don't tell you #3

If multiple indexes can be applied to a WHERE clause, and they all have an equal number of columns specified, only the index created last will be used. For example:

```
SELECT col1, ...
  FROM emp
 WHERE emp_name = 'GURRY'
   AND emp_no   = 127
   AND dept_no  = 12
   AND emp_category = 'CLERK'

Index1 (emp_name, emp_category)  Created 4pm Feb 11th 2002
Index2 (emp_no, dept_no) Created 5pm Feb 11th 2002
```

In this example, only Index2 is used, because it was created at 5 p.m. and the other index was created at 4 p.m. This behavior can pose a problem, because if you rebuild indexes in a different order than they were first created, a different index may suddenly be used for your queries. To deal with this problem, many sites have a naming standard requiring that indexes are named in alphabetical order as they are created. Then, if a table is rebuilt, the indexes can be rebuilt in alphabetical order, preserving the correct creation order. You could, for example, number your indexes. Each new index added to a table would then be given the next number.

What the RBO rules don't tell you #4

If multiple columns of an index are being accessed with an = operator, that will override other operators such as LIKE or BETWEEN. Two ='s will override two ='s and a LIKE. For example:

```
SELECT col1, ...
  FROM emp
 WHERE emp_name   LIKE 'GUR%'
   AND emp_no       = 127
   AND dept_no      = 12
   AND emp_category = 'CLERK'
   AND emp_class    = 'C1'

Index1 (emp_category, emp_class, emp_name)
Index2 (emp_no, dept_no)
```

In this example, only Index2 is utilized despite Index1 having three columns accessed and Index2 having only two column accessed.

What the RBO rules don't tell you #5

A higher percentage of columns accessed will override a lower percentage of columns accessed. So generally, the optimizer will choose to use the index from which you specify the highest percentage of columns. However, as stated previously, all columns specified in a unique or primary key index will override the use of all other indexes. For example:

```
SELECT col1, ...
  FROM emp
 WHERE emp_name  = 'GURRY'
   AND emp_no    = 127
   AND emp_class = 'C1'

Index1 (emp_name, emp_class, emp_category)
Index2 (emp_no, dept_no)
```

In this example, only Index1 is utilized, because 66% of the columns are accessed. Index2 is not used because a lesser 50% of the indexed columns are used.

What the RBO rules don't tell you #6

If you join two tables, the rule-based optimizer needs to select a driving table. The table selected can have a significant impact on performance, particularly when the optimizer decides to use nested loops. A row will be returned from the driving table, and then the matching rows selected from the other table. It is important that as few rows as possible are selected from the driving table.

The rule-based optimizer uses the following rules to select the driving table:

- A unique or primary key index will always cause the associated table to be selected as the driving table in front of a non-unique or non-primary key index.

- An index for which you apply the equality operator (=) to all columns will take precedence over indexes from which you use only some columns, and will result in the underlying table being chosen as the driving table for the query.

- The table that has a higher percentage of columns in an index will override the table that has a lesser percentage of columns indexed.

- A table that satisfies one two-column index in the WHERE clause of a query will be chosen as the driving table in front of a table that satisfies two single-column indexes.

- If two tables have the same number of index columns satisfied, the table that is listed last in the FROM clause will be the driving table. In the SQL below, the EMP table will be the driving table because it is listed last in the FROM clause.

```
SELECT ....
  FROM DEPT d, EMP e
```

```
WHERE e.emp_name    = 'GURRY'
  AND d.dept_name   = 'FINANCE'
  AND d.dept_no     = e.dept_no
```

What the RBO rules don't tell you #7

If a WHERE clause has a column that is the leading column on any index, the rule-based optimizer will use that index. The exception is if a function is placed on the leading index column in the WHERE clause. For example:

```
SELECT col1, ...
  FROM emp
 WHERE emp_name    = 'GURRY'

Index1 (emp_name, emp_class, emp_category)
Index2 (emp_class, emp_name, emp_category)
```

Index1 will be used, because emp_name (used in the WHERE clause) is the leading column. Index2 will not be used, because emp_name is not the leading column.

The following example illustrates what happens when a function is applied to an indexed column:

```
SELECT col1, ...
  FROM emp
 WHERE LTRIM(emp_name) = 'GURRY'
```

In this case, because the LTRIM function has been applied to the column, *no* index will be used.

Understanding the Cost-Based Optimizer

The cost-based optimizer is a more sophisticated facility than the rule-based optimizer. To determine the best execution path for a statement, it uses database information such as table size, number of rows, key spread, and so forth, rather than rigid rules.

The information required by the cost-based optimizer is available once a table has been analyzed via the ANALYZE command, or via the DBMS_STATS facility. If a table has not been analyzed, the cost-based optimizer can use only rule-based logic to select the best access path. It is possible to run a schema with a combination of cost-based and rule-based behavior by having some tables analyzed and others not analyzed.

NOTE

The ANALYZE command and the DBMS_STATS functions collect statistics about tables, clusters, and indexes, and store those statistics in the data dictionary.

A SQL statement will default to the cost-based optimizer if any one of the tables involved in the statement has been analyzed. The cost-based optimizer then makes an educated guess as to the best access path for the other tables based on information in the data dictionary.

The RDBMS kernel defaults to using the cost-based optimizer under a number of situations, including the following:

- OPTIMIZER_MODE = CHOOSE has been specified in the INIT.ORA file, and statistics exist for at least one table involved in the statement

- An ALTER SESSION SET OPTIMIZER_MODE = CHOOSE command has been executed, and statistics exist for at least one table involved in the statement

- An ALTER SESSION SET OPTIMIZER_MODE = FIRST_ROWS (or ALL_ROWS) command has been executed, and statistics exist for at least one table involved in the statement

- A statement uses the FIRST_ROWS or ALL_ROWS hint (e.g., SELECT /*+ FIRST_ROWS */. . .)

ANALYZE command

The way that you analyze your tables can have a dramatic effect on your SQL performance. If your DBA forgets to analyze tables or indexes after a table re-build, the impact on performance can be devastating. If your DBA analyzes each weekend, a new threshold may be reached and Oracle may change its execution plan. The new plan will more often than not be an improvement, but will occasionally be worse.

I cannot stress enough that if every SQL statement has been tuned, do *not* analyze just for the sake of it. One site that I tuned had a critical SQL statement that returned data in less than a second. The DBA analyzed each weekend believing that the execution path would continue to improve. One Monday, morning I got a phone call telling me that the response time had risen to 310 seconds.

If you do want to analyze frequently, use DBMS_STATS. EXPORT_SCHEMA_STATS to back up the existing statistics prior to re-analyzing. This gives you the ability to revert back to the previous statistics if things screw up.

When you analyze, you can have Oracle look at all rows in a table (ANALYZE COMPUTE) or at a sampling of rows (ANALYZE ESTIMATE). Typically, I use ANALYZE ESTIMATE for very large tables (1,000,000 rows or more), and ANALYZE COMPUTE for small to medium tables.

I strongly recommend that you analyze FOR ALL INDEXED COLUMNS for any table that can have severe data skewness. For example, if a large percentage of rows in a table has the same value in a given column, that represents skewness. The FOR ALL INDEXED COLUMNS option makes the cost-based optimizer aware of the skewness of a column's data in addition to the cardinality (number-distinct values) of that data.

When a table is analyzed using ANALYZE, all associated indexes are analyzed as well. If an index is subsequently dropped and recreated, it must be re-analyzed. Be aware that the procedures DBMS_STATS.GATHER_SCHEMA_STATS and GATHER_TABLE_STATS analyze only tables by default, not their indexes. When using those procedures, you must specify the CASCADE=>TRUE option for indexes to be analyzed as well.

Following are some sample ANALYZE statements:

```
ANALYZE TABLE EMP ESTIMATE STATISTICS SAMPLE 5 PERCENT FOR
ALL INDEXED COLUMNS;

ANALYZE INDEX EMP_NDX1 ESTIMATE STATISTICS SAMPLE 5
PERCENT FOR ALL INDEXED COLUMNS;

ANALYZE TABLE EMP COMPUTE STATISTICS FOR ALL INDEXED
COLUMNS;
```

If you analyze a table by mistake, you can delete the statistics. For example:

```
ANALYZE TABLE EMP DELETE STATISTICS;
```

Analyzing can take an excessive amount of time if you use the COMPUTE option on large objects. We find that on almost every occasion, ANALYZE ESTIMATE 5 PERCENT on a large table forces the optimizer make the same decision as ANALYZE COMPUTE.

Tuning prior to releasing to production

A major dilemma that exists with respect to the cost-based optimizer (CBO) is how to tune the SQL for production prior to it being released. Most development and test databases will contain substantially fewer rows than a production database. It is therefore highly likely that the CBO will make different decisions on execution plans. Many sites can't afford the cost and inconvenience of copying the production database into a pre-production database.

Oracle8*i* and later provides various features to overcome this problem, including DBMS_STATS and the outline facility. Each is explained in more detail later in this book.

Inner workings of the cost-based optimizer

Unlike the rule-based optimizer, the cost-based optimizer does not have hard and fast path evaluation rules. The cost-based optimizer is flexible and can adapt to its environment. This adaptation is possible only once the necessary underlying object statistics have been refreshed (re-analyzed). What is constant is the method by which the cost-based optimizer calculates each possible execution plan and evaluates its cost (efficiency).

The cost-based optimizer's functionality can be (loosely) broken into the following steps:

1. Parse the SQL (check syntax, object privileges, etc.).
2. Generate a list of *all* potential execution plans.
3. Calculate (estimate) the cost of each execution plan using all available object statistics.
4. Select the execution plan with the lowest cost.

The cost-based optimizer will be used only if at least one table within a SQL statement has statistics (table statistics for unanalyzed tables are estimated). If no statistics are available for any table involved in the SQL, the RDBMS will resort to the rule-based optimizer, unless the cost-based optimizer is forced via statement-level HINTS or by an optimizer goal of ALL_ROWS or FIRST_ROWS.

To understand how the cost-based optimizer works and, ultimately, how to exploit it, we need to understand how it thinks.

Primary key and/or UNIQUE index equality
> A UNIQUE index's selectivity is recognized as 100%. No other indexed access method is more precise. For this reason, a unique index is always used when available.

Non-UNIQUE index equality
> For non-UNIQUE indexes, index selectivity is calculated. The cost-based optimizer makes the assumption

that the table (and subsequent indexes) have uniform data spread unless you use the FOR ALL INDEXED COLUMNS option of the ANALYZE. That option will make the cost-based optimizer aware of how the data in the indexed columns is skewed.

Range evaluation

For index range execution plans, selectivity is evaluated. This evaluation is based on a column's most recent high-value and low-value statistics. Again, the cost-based optimizer makes the assumption that the table (and subsequent indexes) have uniform data spread unless you use the FOR ALL INDEXED COLUMNS option when analyzing the table.

Range evaluation over bind variables

For index range execution plans, selectivity is guessed. Prior to Oracle9*i*, because bind variable values are not available at parse time (values are passed to the cursor after the execution plan has been decided), the optimizer cannot make decisions based on bind variable values. The optimizer assumes a rule of thumb of 25% selectivity for unbounded bind variable ranges (e.g., WHERE dept_no = :b1) and 50% selectivity for bounded ranges (WHERE dept_no > :b1 AND dept_no < :b2). Beginning with Oracle9*i*, the cost-based optimizer obtains bind variable values prior to determining an execution plan.

Histograms

Prior to the introduction of histograms in Oracle 7.3, The cost-based optimizer could not distinguish grossly uneven key data spreads.

System resource usage

By default, the cost-based optimizer assumes that you are the only person accessing the database. Oracle9*i* gives you the ability to store information about system resource usage, and can make much better informed

decisions based on workload (read up on the DBMS_
STATS.GATHER_SYSTEM_STATS package).

Current statistics are important

The cost-based optimizer can make poor execution plan choices when a table has been analyzed but its indexes have not been, or when indexes have been analyzed but not the tables.

You should not force the database to use the cost-based optimizer via inline hints when no statistics are available for any table involved in the SQL.

Using old (obsolete) statistics can be more dangerous than estimating the statistics at runtime, but keep in mind that changing statistics frequently can also blow up in your face, particularly on a mission-critical system with lots of online users. Always back up your statistics before you re-analyze by using DBMS_STATS.EXPORT_SCHEMA_STATS.

Analyzing large tables and their associated indexes with the COMPUTE option will take a long, long time, requiring lots of CPU, I/O, and temporary tablespace resources. It is often overkill. Analyzing with a consistent value, for example, estimate 3%, will usually allow the cost-based optimizer to make optimal decisions

Combining the information provided by the selectivity rules with other database I/O information allows the cost-based optimizer to calculate the cost of an execution plan.

EXPLAIN PLAN for the cost-based optimizer

Oracle provides information on the cost of query execution via the EXPLAIN PLAN facility. EXPLAIN PLAN can be used to display the calculated execution cost(s) via some extensions to the utility. In particular, the plan table's COST column returns a value that increases or decreases to show the relative cost of a query. For example:

```
EXPLAIN PLAN FOR
  SELECT count(*)
    FROM winners, horses
   WHERE winners.owner=horses.owner
     AND winners.horse_name LIKE 'Mr %'

COLUMN "SQL" FORMAT a56

SELECT lpad(' ',2*level)||operation||''
       ||options ||' '||object_name||
       decode(OBJECT_TYPE, '', '',
         '('||object_type||')') "SQL",
       cost "Cost", cardinality "Num Rows"
  FROM   plan_table
CONNECT BY prior id = parent_id
  START WITH id = 0;
```

```
SQL                                  Cost   Num Rows
-------------------------------------------------------
SELECT STATEMENT                       44          1
  SORT AGGREGATE
    HASH JOIN                          44     100469
      INDEX RANGE SCAN MG1(NON-UNIQUE)
                                        2       1471
      INDEX FAST FULL SCAN OWNER_PK(UNIQUE)
                                        4       6830
```

By manipulating the cost-based optimizer (i.e., via inline hints, by creating/removing indexes, or by adjusting the way that indexes or tables are analyzed), we can see the differences in the execution cost as calculated by the optimizer. Use EXPLAIN PLAN to look at different variations on a query, and choose the variation with the lowest relative cost.

For absolute optimal performance, many sites have the majority of the tables and indexes analyzed but a small number of tables that are used in isolation are not analyzed. This is usually to force rule-based behavior on the tables that are not analyzed. However, it is important that tables that have not been analyzed are not joined with tables that have been analyzed.

Some Common Optimizer Misconceptions

Let's clear up some common misconceptions regarding the optimizers:

Oracle8i and Oracle9i don't support the rule-based optimizer
This is totally false. Certain publications mentioned this some time ago, but Oracle now assures us that this is definitely *not* true.

Hints can't be used with the rule-based optimizer
The large majority of hints can indeed be applied to SQL statements using the rule-based optimizer.

SQL tuned for rule will run well in cost
If you are very lucky it may, but when you transfer to cost, expect a handful of SQL statements that require tuning. However, there is not a single site that I have transferred and been unable to tune.

SQL tuned for cost will run well in rule
This is highly unlikely, unless the code was written with knowledge of the rule-based optimizer.

You can't run rule and cost together
You can run both together by setting the INIT.ORA parameter OPTIMIZER_MODE to CHOOSE, and having some tables analyzed and others not. Be careful that you don't join tables that *are* analyzed with tables that are *not* analyzed.

Which Optimizer to Use?

If you are currently using the rule-based optimizer, I strongly recommend that you transfer to the cost-based optimizer. Here is a list of the reasons why:

- The time spent coding is reduced.
- Coders do not need to be aware of the rules.
- There are more features, and far more tuning tools, available for the cost-based optimizer.

- The chances of third-party packages performing well has been improved considerably. Many third-party packages are written to run on DB2, Informix, and SQL*Server, as well as on Oracle. The code has *not* been written to suit the rule-based optimizer; it has been written in a generic fashion.

- End users can develop tuned code without having to learn a large set of optimizer rules.

- The cost-based optimizer has improved dramatically from one version of Oracle to the next. Development of the rule-based optimizer is stalled.

- There is less risk from adding new indexes.

- There are many features that are available only with the cost-based optimizer. These features include recognition of materialized views, star transformation, the use of function indexes, and so on. The number of such features is huge, and as time goes on, the gap between cost and rule will widen.

- Oracle has introduced features such as the DBMS_STATS package and outlines to get around known problems with the inconsistency of the cost-based optimizer across environments.

Rule-Based Optimizer Problems and Solutions

The rule-based optimizer provides a good deal of scope for tuning. Because its behavior is predictable, and governed by the 20 condition rankings presented earlier in Table 1, we are easily able to manipulate its choices.

I have been tracking the types of problems that occur with both optimizers as well as the best way of fixing the problems. The major causes of poor rule-based optimizer performance are shown in Table 2.

Table 2. Common rule-based optimizer problems

Problem	% Cases
1. Incorrect driving table	40%
2. Incorrect index	40%
3. Incorrect driving index	10%
4. Using the ORDER BY index and not the WHERE index	10%

Each problem, along with its solution, is explained in detail in the following sections.

Problem 1: Incorrect Driving Table

If the table driving a join is not optimal, there can be a significant increase in the amount of time required to execute a query. Earlier, in the section "What the RBO rules don't tell you #6," I discussed what decides the driving table. Consider the following example, which illustrates the potential difference in runtimes:

```
SELECT COUNT(*)
  FROM acct a, trans b
 WHERE b.cost_center = 'MASS'
   AND a.acct_name = 'MGA'
   AND a.acct_name = b.acct_name;
```

In this example, if ACCT_NAME represents a unique key index and COST_CENTER represents a single column non-unique index, the unique key index would make the ACCT table the driving table.

If both COST_CENTER and ACCT_NAME were single column, non-unique indexes, the rule-based optimizer would select the TRANS table as the driving table, because it is listed last in the FROM clause. Having the TRANS table as the driving table would likely mean a longer response time for a query, because there is usually only one ACCT row for a selected account name but there are likely to be many transactions for a given cost center.

With the rule-based optimizer, if the index rankings are identical for both tables, Oracle simply executes the statement in the order in which the tables are parsed. Because the parser processes table names from right to left, the table name that is specified *last* (e.g., DEPT in the example above) is actually the *first* table processed (the driving table).

```
SELECT COUNT(*)
  FROM acct a, trans b
 WHERE  b.cost_center = 'MASS'
   AND  a.acct_name = 'MGA'
   AND  a.acct_name = b.acct_name;
```

Response = 19.722 seconds

The response time following the re-ordering of the tables in the FROM clause is as follows:

```
SELECT COUNT(*)
  FROM trans b, acct a
 WHERE  b.cost_center= 'MASS'
   AND  a.acct_name = 'MGA'
   AND  a.acct_name = b.acct_name;
```

Response = 1.904 seconds

It is important that the table that is listed last in the FROM clause is going to return the fewest number of rows. There is also potential to adjust your indexing to force the driving table. For example, you may be able to make the COST_CENTER index a concatenated index, joined with another column that is frequently used in SQL enquires with the column. This will avoid it ranking so highly when joins take place.

Problem 2: Incorrect Index

WHERE clauses often provide the rule-based optimizer with a number of indexes that it could utilize. The rule-based optimizer is totally unaware of how many rows each index will be required to scan and the potential impact on the response

---

time. A poor index selection will provide a response time much greater than it would be if a more effective index was selected.

The rule-based optimizer has simple rules for selecting which index to use. These rules and scenarios are described earlier in the various "What the RBO rules don't tell you" sections.

Let's consider an example.

An ERP package has been developed in a generic fashion to allow a site to use columns for reporting purposes in any way its users please. There is a column called BUSINESS_UNIT that has a single-column index on it. Most sites have hundreds of business units. Other sites have only one business unit.

Our JOURNAL table has an index on (BUSINESS_UNIT), and another on (BUSINESS_UNIT, ACCOUNT, JOURNAL_DATE). The WHERE clause of a query is as follows:

```
WHERE business_unit  ='A203'
   AND account         = 801919
   AND journal_date between
       '01-DEC-2001'    and '31-DEC-2001'
```

The single-column index will be used in preference to the three-column index, despite the fact that the three-column index returns the result in a fraction of the time of the single-column index. This is because *all* columns in the single-column index are used in the query. In such a situation, the only options open to us are to drop the index or use the cost-based optimizer. If you're not using packaged software, you may also be able to use hints.

Problem 3: Incorrect Driving Index

The way you specify conditions in the WHERE clause(s) of your SELECT statements has a major impact on the performance of your SQL, because the order in which you specify conditions impacts the indexes the optimizer choose to use.

If two index rankings are equal—for example, two single-column indexes both have their columns in the WHERE clause—Oracle will merge the indexes. The merge (AND-EQUAL) order has the potential to have a significant impact on runtime. If the index that drives the query returns more rows than the other index, query performance will be sub-optimal. The effect is very similar to that from the ordering of tables in the FROM clause. Consider the following example:

```
SELECT COUNT(*)
  FROM trans
 WHERE  cost_center = 'MASS'
   AND  bmark_id     = 9;
```

Response Time = 4.255 seconds

The index that has the column that is listed first in the WHERE CLAUSE will drive the query. In this statement, the indexed entries for COST_CENTER = 'MASS' will return significantly more rows than those for BMARK_ID=9, which will return at most only one or two rows.

The following query reverses the order of the conditions in the WHERE clause, resulting in a much faster execution time.

```
SELECT COUNT(*)
    FROM trans
 WHERE  bmark_id     = 9
   AND  cost_center = 'MASS';
```

Response Time = 1.044 seconds

For the rule-based optimizer, you should order the conditions that are going to return the fewest number of rows higher in your WHERE clause.

Problem 4: Using the ORDER BY Index and not the WHERE Index

A less common problem with index selection, which we have observed at sites using the rule-based optimizer, is illustrated by the following query and indexes:

```
SELECT fod_flag, account_no...
  FROM account_master
 WHERE (account_code like 'I%')
  ORDER BY account_no;

Index_1 UNIQUE (ACCOUNT_NO)
Index_2        (ACCOUNT_CODE)
```

With the indexes shown, the runtime of this query was 20 minutes. The query was used for a report, which was run by many brokers each day.

In this example, the optimizer is trying to avoid a sort, and has opted for the index that contains the column in the ORDER BY clause rather than for the index that has the column in the WHERE clause.

The site that experienced this particular problem was a large stock brokerage. The SQL was run frequently to produce account financial summaries.

This problem was repaired by creating a concatenated index on both columns:

```
# Added Index (ACCOUNT_CODE, ACCOUNT_NO)
```

We decided to drop index_2 (ACCOUNT CODE), which was no longer required because the ACCOUNT_CODE was the leading column of the new index. The ACCOUNT_NO column was added to the new index to take advantage of the index storing the data in ascending order. Having the ACCOUNT_NO column in the index avoided the need to sort, adding the index in a runtime of under 10 seconds.

Cost-Based Optimizer Problems and Solutions

The cost-based optimizer has been significantly improved from its initial inception. My recommendation is that every site that is new to Oracle should be using the cost-based optimizer. I also recommend that sites currently using the rule-based optimizer have a plan in place for migrating to the cost-based optimizer. There are, however, some issues with the cost-based optimizer that you should be aware of. Table 3 lists the most common problems I have observed, along with their frequency of occurrence.

Table 3. Common cost-based optimizer problems

Problem	% Cases
1. The skewness problem	30%
2. Analyzing with wrong data	25%
3. Mixing the optimizers in joins	20%
4. Choosing an inferior index	20%
5. Joining too many tables	< 5%
6. Incorrect INIT.ORA parameter settings	< 5%

Problem 1: The Skewness Problem

Imagine that we are consulting at a site with a table TRANS that has a column called STATUS. The column has two possible values: 'O' for Open Transactions that have not been posted, and 'C' for closed transactions that have already been posted and that require no further action. There are over one million rows that have a status of 'C', but only 100 rows that have a status of 'O' at any point in time.

The site has the following SQL statement that runs many hundreds of times daily. The response time is dismal, and we have been called in to "make it go faster."

```
SELECT acct_no, customer, product, trans_date, amt
  FROM trans
 WHERE status='O';
```

Response time = 16.308 seconds

In this example, taken from a real-life client of mine, the cost-based optimizer decides that Oracle should perform a full table scan. This is because the cost-based optimizer is aware of how many distinct values there are for the status column, but is unaware of how many rows exist for each of those values. Consequently, the optimizer assumes a 50/50 spread of data for each of the two values, 'O' and 'C'. Given this assumption, Oracle has decided to perform a full table scan to retrieve open transactions.

If we inform Oracle of the data skewness by specifying the option FOR ALL INDEXED COLUMNS when we run the ANALYZE command or when we invoke the DBMS_STATS package, Oracle will be made aware of the skewness of the data; that is, the number of rows that exist for each value for each indexed column. In our scenario, the STATUS column is indexed. The following command is used to analyze the table:

```
ANALYZE TABLE TRANS COMPUTE STATISTICS
        FOR ALL INDEXED COLUMNS
```

After analyzing the table and computing statistics for all indexed columns, the cost-based optimizer is aware that there are only 100 or so rows with a status of 'O', and it will accordingly use the index on that column. Use of the index on the STATUS column results in the following, much faster, query response:

Response Time: 0.259 seconds

Typically the cost-based optimizer will perform a full table scan if the value selected for a column has over 12% of the rows in the table, and will use the index if the value specified has less than 12% of the rows. The cost-based optimizer selections are not quite as firm as this, but as a rule of thumb this is the typical behavior that the cost-based optimizer will follow.

Prior to Oracle9i, if a statement has been written to use bind variables, problems can still occur with respect to skewness even if you use FOR ALL INDEXED COLUMNS. Consider the following example:

```
local_status := '0';

SELECT acct_no, customer, product, trans_date, amt
  FROM trans
WHERE status= local_status;
```

 # Response time = 16.608

Notice that the response time is similar to that experienced when the FOR ALL INDEXED columns option was not used. The problem here is that the cost-based optimizer isn't aware of the value of the bind variable when it generates an execution plan. As a general rule, to overcome the skewness problem, you should do the following:

- Hardcode literals if possible. For example, use WHERE STATUS = 'O', not WHERE STATUS = local_status.
- Always analyze with the option FOR ALL INDEXED COLUMNS.

If you are still experiencing performance problems in which the cost-based optimizer will not use an index due to bind variables being used, and you can't change the source code, you can try deleting the statistics off the index using a command such as the following:

```
ANALYZE INDEX
TRANS_STATUS_NDX
DELETE STATISTICS
```

Deleting the index statistics works because it forces rule-based optimizer behavior, which will always use the existing indexes (as opposed to doing full table scans).

Problem 2: Analyzing with Wrong Data

I have been invited to many, many sites that have performance problems at which I quickly determined that the tables and indexes were not analyzed at a time when they contained typical volumes of data. The cost-based optimizer requires accurate information, including accurate data volumes, to have any chance of creating efficient execution plans.

The times when the statistics are most likely to be forgotten or out of date are when a table is rebuilt or moved, an index is added, or a new environment is created. For example, a DBA might forget to regenerate statistics after migrating a database schema to a production environment. Other problems typically occur when the DBA does not have a solid knowledge of the database that he/she is dealing with and analyzes a table when it has zero rows, instead of when it has hundreds of thousands of rows shortly afterwards.

How to check the last analyzed date

To observe which tables, indexes, and partitions have been analyzed, and when they were last analyzed, you can select the LAST_ANALYZED column from the various user_XXX view. For example, to determine the last analyzed date for all your tables:

```
SELECT table_name, num_rows,
       last_analyzed
  FROM user_tables;
```

In addition to user_tables, there are many other views you can select to view the date an object was last analyzed. To

---

obtain a full list of views with LAST_ANALYZED dates, run the following query:

```
SELECT table_name
  FROM all_tab_columns
 WHERE column_name = 'LAST_ANALYZED'
```

This is not to say that you should be analyzing with the COMPUTE option as often as possible. Analyzing frequently can cause a tuned SQL statement to become untuned.

When to analyze

Re-analyzing tables and indexes can be almost as dangerous as adjusting your indexing, and should ideally be tested in a copy of the production database prior to being applied to the production database.

Peoplesoft software is one example of an application that uses temporary holding tables, with the table names typically ending with _TMP. When batch processing commences, each holding table will usually have zero rows. As each stage of the batch process completes, insertions and updates are happening against the holding tables.

The final stages of the batch processing populate the major Peoplesoft transaction tables by extracting data from the holding tables. When a batch run completes, all rows are usually deleted from the holding tables. Transactions against the holding tables are not committed until the end of a batch run, when there are no rows left in the table.

When you run ANALYZE on the temporary holding tables, they will usually have zero rows. When the cost-based optimizer sees zero rows, it immediately considers full table scans and Cartesian joins. To overcome this issue, I suggest that you populate the holding tables, and analyze them with data in them. You can then truncate the tables and commence normal processing. When you truncate a table, the statistics are not removed.

You can find INSERT and UPDATE SQL statements to use in populating the holding tables by tracing the batch process that usually populates and updates the tables. You can use the same SQL to populate the tables.

The runtimes of the batch jobs at one large Peoplesoft site in Australia went from over 36 hours down to under 30 minutes using this approach.

If analyzing temporary holding tables with production data volumes does not alleviate performance problems, consider removing the statistics from those tables. This forces SQL statements against the tables to use rule-based optimizer behavior. You can delete statistics using the ANALYZE TABLE *tname* DELETE STATISTICS command. If the statistics are removed, it is important that you not allow the tables to join with tables that have valid statistics. It is also important that indexes that have statistics are not used to resolve any queries against the unanalyzed tables. If the temporary tables are used in isolation, and only joined with each other, the rule-based behavior is often preferable to that of the cost-based optimizer.

Problem 3: Mixing the Optimizers in Joins

As mentioned in the previous section, when tables are being joined, and one table in the join is analyzed and the other tables are not, the cost-based optimizer performs at its worst.

When you analyze your tables and indexes using the DBMS_STATS.GATHER_SCHEMA_STATS procedure and the GATHER_TABLE_STATS procedures, be careful to include the CASCADE>=TRUE option. By default, the DBMS_STATS package will gather statistics for tables only. Having statistics on the tables, and not on their indexes, can also cause the cost-based optimizer to make poor execution plan decisions.

One example of this problem that I experienced recently was at a site that had a TRANS table not analyzed, and an ACCT table analyzed. The DBA had rebuilt the TRANS table to purge data, and had simply forgotten to do the analyze afterwards. The following example shows the performance of a query joining the two tables:

```
SELECT a.account_name, sum(b.amount)
   FROM trans b, acct a
  WHERE b.trans_date > sysdate - 7
     AND a.acct_id   = b.acct_ID
     AND a.acct_status = 'A'
  GROUP BY account_name;

SORT GROUP BY
    NESTED LOOPS
        TABLE ACCESS BY ROWID ACCT
            INDEX UNIQUE SCAN ACCT_PK
        TABLE ACCESS FULL TRANS
```

Response Time = 410 seconds

After the TRANS table was analyzed using the following command, the response time for the query was reduced by a large margin:

```
ANALYZE TABLE trans ESTIMATE STATISTICS
    SAMPLE 3 PERCENT
    FOR ALL INDEXED COLUMNS
```

The new execution plan, and response time, were as follows:

```
SORT GROUP BY
    NESTED LOOPS
        TABLE ACCESS BY ROWID ACCT
            INDEX UNIQUE SCAN ACCT_PK
        TABLE ACCESS BY ROWID TRANS
            INDEX RANGE SCAN TRANS_NDX1
```

Response Time = 3.1 seconds

One other site that I was asked to tune had been instructed by the vendor of their personnel package to ANALYZE only their indexes and not their tables. The software provider had developed the software for Microsoft's SQL Server database, and had ported it to Oracle. The results of just analyzing the indexes caused widespread devastation. For example:

```
SELECT count(*)
   FROM trans
WHERE acct_id = 9
    AND cost_center = 'VIC';

TRANS_IDX2 is on ACCT_ID
TRANS_NDX3 is on COST_CENTER
```

Response Time 77.3 Seconds

Ironically, the software developers were blaming Oracle, claiming that it had inferior performance to SQL Server. After analyzing the tables and indexes, the response time of this SQL statement was dramatically improved to 0.415 seconds. The response times for many, many other SQL statements were also dramatically improved.

The moral of this story could be to let Oracle tuning experts tune Oracle and have SQL Server experts stick to SQL Server. However, with ever more mobile and cross-database trained IT professionals, I would suggest that we all take more care in reading the manuals when we tackle the tuning of a new database.

Problem 4: Choosing an Inferior Index

The cost-based optimizer will sometimes choose an inferior index, despite it appearing obvious that another index should be used. Consider the following Peoplesoft WHERE clause:

```
where business_unit      = :5
   and ledger            = :6
   and fiscal_year       = :7
   and accounting_period = :8
   and affiliate         = :9
   and statistics_code   = :10
   and project_id        = :11
   and account           = :12
   and currency_cd       = :13
   and deptid            = :14
   and product           = :15
```

The Peoplesoft system from which I took this example had an index that had every single column in the WHERE clause contained within it. It would seem that Oracle would definitely use that index when executing the query. Instead, the cost-based optimizer decided to use an index on (BUSINESS_UNIT, LEDGER, FISCAL_YEAR, ACCOUNT). We extracted the SQL statement and compared its runtime to that when using a hint to force the use of the larger index. The runtime when using the index containing all the columns was over four times faster than the runtime obtained when using the index chosen by the cost-based optimizer.

After further investigation, we observed that the index should have been created as a UNIQUE index, but had mistakenly been created as a non-UNIQUE index as part of a data purge and table rebuild. When the index was rebuilt as a unique index, the index was used. The users were obviously happy with their four-fold performance improvement.

However, more headaches were to come. The same index was the ideal candidate for the following statement, which was one of the statements run frequently during end-of-month and end-of-year processing:

```
where business_unit      = :5
  and ledger             = :6
  and fiscal_year        = :7
  and accounting_period between 1 and 12
  and affiliate          = :9
  and statistics_code    = :10
  and project_id         = :11
  and account            = :12
  and currency_cd        = :13
  and deptid             = :14
  and product            = :15
```

Despite the index being correctly created as UNIQUE, the cost-based optimizer was once again ignoring it. The only difference between this statement and the last is that this statement is after a *range* of accounting periods for the financial year rather than just one accounting period.

This WHERE clause used the same incorrect index as previously mentioned, with the columns (BUSINESS_UNIT, LEDGER, FISCAL_YEAR, and ACCOUNT). Once again, we timed the statement using the index selected by the cost-based optimizer against the index that contained all of the columns, and found the larger index to be at least three times faster.

The problem was overcome by repositioning the ACCOUNTING_PERIOD column (originally third in the index) to be last in the index. The new index order was as follows:

```
business_unit
ledger
fiscal_year
affiliate
statistics_code
project_id
account
currency_cd
deptid
Product
accounting_period
```

Another way to force the cost-based optimizer to use an index is to use one of the hints that allows you to specify an index. This is fine, but often sites are using third-party packages that can't be modified, and consequently hints can't be utilized. However, there may be the potential to create a view that contains a hint, with users then accessing the view. A view is useful if the SQL that is performing badly is from a report or online inquiry that is able to read from views.

As a last resort, I have discovered that sometimes, to force the use of an index, you can delete the statistics on the index. Occasionally you can also ANALYZE ESTIMATE with just the basic 1,064 rows being analyzed. Often, the execution plan will change to just the way you want it, but this type of practice is approaching black magic. It is critical that if you adopt such a black magic approach, you clearly document what you have done to improve performance. Yet another method to try is lowering the OPTIMIZER_INDEX_COST_ADJ parameter to between 10 and 50.

In summary, why does the cost-based optimizer make such poor decisions? First of all, I must point out that poor decision-making is the exception rather than the rule. The examples in this section indicate that columns are looked at individually rather than as a group. If they were looked at as a group, the cost-based optimizer would have realized in the first example that each row looked at was unique without the DBA having to rebuild the index as unique. The second example illustrates that if several of the columns in an index have a low number of distinct values, and the SQL is requesting most of those values, the cost-based optimizer will often bypass the index. This happens despite the fact that collectively, the columns are very specific and will return very few rows.

In fairness to the optimizer, queries using indexes with fewer columns will often perform substantially faster than those using an index with many columns.

Problem 5: Joining Too Many Tables

Early versions of the cost-based optimizer often adopted a divide and conquer approach when more than five tables were joined. Consider the example shown in Figure 1. The query is selecting all related data for a company whose account ID (in the ACCT_ID column) is equal to 777818. The company has several branches, and the request is just for the branches in Washington State (WA). The A table is the ACCT table, the F table is ACCT_ADDRESS, and the G table is the ADDRESS table.

The query expects to return just a handful of rows from the various tables, and the response time should be no longer than one second. Ideally, Oracle receives the ACCT_ADDRESS rows for the relevant account, and then joins to

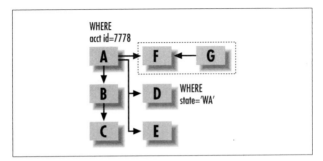

Figure 1. A join of seven tables

the ADDRESS table to determine if the addresses are in Washington.

However, because so many tables are being joined, the cost-based optimizer will often process F and G independently of the other tables and then merge the data at the end. The result of joining F and G first is that all address that are in the state of Washington must be selected. That process could take several minutes, causing the overall runtime to be far beyond what it would have been if Oracle had driven all table accesses from the A table.

Assuming you have an ACCT_ID index on the ACCT_ADDRESS (F) table, you can often overcome this problem by placing a hint to tell the cost-based optimizer to use that index. This will speed the performance significantly.

Interestingly, the rule-based optimizer often makes a bigger mess of the execution plan when many tables are joined than does the cost-based optimizer. The rule-based optimizer often will not use the ACCT table as the driving table. To assist the rule-based optimizer, place the A table last in the FROM clause.

If you are using a third-party package, your best option may be to create a view with a hint, if that is allowable and possible with the package you are using.

Problem 6: Incorrect INIT.ORA Parameter Settings

Many sites utilize a pre-production database to test SQL performance prior to moving index and code changes through to production. Ideally the pre-production database will have production volumes of data, and will have the tables analyzed in exactly the same way as the production database. The pre-production database will often be a copy of the actual production datafiles.

When DBAs test changes in pre-production, they may work fine, but have problems with a different execution plan being used in production. How can this be? The reason for a different execution plan in production is often that there are different parameter settings in the production INIT.ORA file than in the pre-production INIT.ORA file.

I was at one site that ran the following update command and got a four-minute response, despite the fact that the statement's WHERE clause condition referenced the table's primary key. Oddly, if we *selected* from the ACCT table rather than updating it, using the same WHERE clause, the index *was* used.

```
UPDATE acct SET proc_flag = 'Y'
   WHERE pkey=100;

# Response Time took 4 minutes and
# wouldn't use the primary key
```

We tried re-analyzing the table every which way, and eventually removed the statistics. The statement performed well when the statistics were removed and the rule-based optimizer was used.

After much investigation, we decided to check the INIT.ORA parameters. We discovered that the COMPATIBLE parameter was set to 8.0.0 despite the database version being Oracle 8.1.7. We decided to set COMPATIBLE to 8.1.7, and, to our delight, the UPDATE statement correctly used the index and ran in about 0.1 seconds.

COMPATIBLE is not the only parameter that needs to be set the same in pre-production as in production to ensure that the cost-based optimizer makes consistent decisions. Other parameters include the following:

SORT_AREA_SIZE
The number of bytes allocated on a per-user session basis to sort data in memory. If the parameter is set at its default of 64K, NESTED LOOPS will be favored instead of SORT MERGES and HASH JOINS.

HASH_AREA_SIZE
The number of bytes to use on a per-user basis to perform hash joins in memory. The default is twice the SORT_AREA_SIZE. Hash joins often will not work unless this parameter is set to at least 1 megabyte.

HASH_JOIN_ENABLED
Enables or disables the usage of hash joins. It has a default of TRUE, and usually doesn't need to be set.

OPTIMIZER_MODE
May be CHOOSE, FIRST_ROWS, or ALL_ROWS. CHOOSE causes the cost-based optimizer to be used if statistics exist. FIRST_ROWS will operate the same way, but will tend to favor NESTED LOOPS instead of SORT MERGE or HASH JOINS. ALL_ROWS will favor SORT MERGEs and HASH JOINS in preference to NESTED LOOP joins.

DB_FILE_MULTIBLOCK_READ_COUNT
The number of blocks that Oracle will retrieve with each read of the table. If you specify a large value, such as 16 or 32, Oracle will, in many cases, bias towards FULL TABLE SCANS instead of NESTED LOOPS.

OPTIMIZER_MODE_ENABLE

Enables new optimizer features to be enabled. For example, setting the parameter to 8.1.7 will enable all of the optimizer features up to and including Oracle 8.1.7. This parameter can also automatically enable other parameters such as FAST_FULL_SCAN_ENABLED.

Some of the major improvements that have occurred with the various Oracle versions include: **8.0.4** (ordered nested loops, fast full scans), **8.0.5** (many, many optimizer bug fixes), **8.1.6** (improved histograms, partitions, and nested loop processing), **8.1.7** (improved partition handling and subexpression optimization), and **9.0.1** (much improved index joins, complex view merging, bitmap improvements, subquery improvements, and push join predicate improvements).

OPTIMIZER_INDEX_CACHING

Tells Oracle the percentage of index data that is expected to be found in memory. This parameter defaults to 0, with a range of 0 to 100. The higher the value, the more likely that NESTED LOOPS will be used in preference to SORT MERGE and HASH JOINs. Some sites have reported performance improvements when this parameter is set to 90.

OPTIMIZER_INDEX_COST_ADJ

This parameter can be set to encourage the use of indexes. It has a default of 100. If you lower the parameter to 10, you are telling the cost-based optimizer to lower the cost of index usage to 10% of its usual value. You can also set the value to something way beyond 100 to force a SORT MERGE or a HASH JOIN. Sites report performance improvements when the parameter is set to between 10 and 50 for OLTP and 50 for decision support systems. Adjusting it downwards may speed up some OLTP enquiries, but make overnight jobs run forever. If you increase its value, the reverse may occur.

STAR_TRANSFORMATION_ENABLED

Causes a star transformation to be used to combine bit-map indexes on fact table columns. This is different from the Cartesian join that usually occurs for star queries.

QUERY_REWRITE_ENABLED

Allows the use of function-based indexes as well as allowing query rewrites for materialized views. The default is FALSE, which may explain why your function indexes are not being used. Set it to TRUE.

PARTITION_VIEW_ENABLED

Enables the use of partition views. If you are utilizing partitioned views, you will have to set this parameter to TRUE because the default is FALSE. A partition view is basically a view that has a UNION ALL join of tables. Partition views were the predecessor to Oracle partitions, and are used very successfully by many sites for archiving and to speed performance.

PARALLEL_BROADCAST_ENABLED

This parameter is used by parallel query when small lookup tables are involved. It has a default of FALSE. If set to TRUE, the rows of small tables are sent to each slave process to speed MERGE JOIN and HASH JOIN times when joining a small table to a larger table.

OPTIMIZER_MAX_PERMUTATIONS

Can be used to reduce parse times. However, reducing the permutations can cause an inefficient execution plan, so this parameter should *not* be modified from its default setting.

CURSOR_SHARING

If set to FORCE or SIMILAR, can result in faster parsing, reduced memory usage in the shared pool, and reduced latch contention. This is achieved by translating similar statements that contain literals in the WHERE clause into statements that have bind variables.

The default is EXACT. We suggest that you consider setting this parameter to SIMILAR with Oracle9i *only* if you are certain that there are lots of similar statements with the only differences between them being the values in the literals. It is far better to write your application to use bind variables if you can.

Setting the parameter to FORCE causes the similar statements to use the same SQL area, which can degrade performance. FORCE should *not* be used.

Note that STAR TRANSFORMATION will *not* work if this parameter is set to SIMILAR or FORCE.

ALWAYS_SEMI_JOIN

This parameter can make a dramatic improvement to applications that make heavy use of WHERE EXISTS. Setting this parameter to MERGE or HASH has caused queries to run in only minutes whereas before they had used up hours of runtime. The default is STANDARD, which means that the main query (not the subquery) drives the execution plan. If you specifically set this parameter, the subquery becomes the driving query.

ALWAYS_ANTI_JOIN

This parameter will change the behavior of NOT IN statements, and can speed processing considerably if set to HASH or MERGE. Setting the parameter causes a merge or hash join rather than the ugly and time-consuming Cartesian join that will occur with standard NOT IN execution.

Remember that if any of these parameters are different in your pre-production database than in your production database, it is possible that the execution plans for your SQL statements will be different. Make the parameters identical to ensure consistent behavior.

Problems Common to Rule and Cost with Solutions

This section lists problems that are common to both the rule-based and cost-based optimizers. It is important that you are aware of these problems and avoid them wherever possible. Table 4 lists the problems and their occurrence rates.

Table 4. Common problems with both optimizers

Problems for both Rule and Cost	Occurrence %
1. Statement not written for indexes	25%
2. Indexes are missing or inappropriate	16%
3. Use of single-column index merge	15%
4. Misuse of nested loop, sort merge, or hash join	12%
5. Misuse of IN, EXISTS, NOT IN, NOT EXISTS, or table joins	8%
6. Unnecessary Sorts	4%
7. Too many indexes on a table	4%
8. Use of OR instead of UNION	3%
9. Tables and indexes with many deletes	3%
10. Other	10%

Problem 1: Statement Not Written for Indexes

Some SELECT statement WHERE clauses do not use indexes at all. Most such problems are caused by having a function on an indexed column. Oracle8*i* and later allow function-based indexes, which may provide an alternative method of using an effective index.

In the examples in this section, for each clause that cannot use an index, I have suggested an alternative approach that will allow you to get better performance out of your SQL statements.

In the following example, the SUBSTR function disables the index when it is used over an indexed column.

Do not use:

```
SELECT account_name, trans_date, amount
FROM   transaction
WHERE  SUBSTR(account_name,1,7) = 'CAPITAL';
```

Use:

```
SELECT account_name, trans_date, amount
FROM   transaction
WHERE  account_name LIKE 'CAPITAL%';
```

In the following example, the != (not equal) function cannot use an index. Remember that indexes can tell you what is in a table but not what is *not in* a table. All references to NOT, !=, and <> disable index usage.

Do not use:

```
SELECT account_name,trans_date,amount
FROM   transaction
WHERE  amount != 0;
```

Use:

```
SELECT account_name,trans_date,amount
FROM   transaction
WHERE  amount > 0 ;
```

In the following example, the TRUNC function disables the index.

Do not use:

```
SELECT account_name, trans_date, amount
FROM   transaction
WHERE  TRUNC(trans_date) = TRUNC(SYSDATE);
```

Use:

```
SELECT account_name, trans_date, amount
FROM   transaction
WHERE  trans_date BETWEEN TRUNC(SYSDATE)
         AND TRUNC(SYSDATE) + .99999;
```

In the following example, || is the *concatenate* function; it strings two character columns together. Like other functions, it disables indexes.

Do not use:

```
SELECT account_name, trans_date, amount
FROM   transaction
WHERE  account_name || account_type = 'AMEXA';
```

Use:

```
SELECT account_name, trans_date, amount
FROM   transaction
WHERE  account_name ='AMEX'
AND    account_type = 'A' ;
```

In the following example, the addition operator is also a function and disables the index. All the other arithmetic operators (-, *, and /) have the same effect.

Do not use:

```
SELECT account_name, trans_date, amount
FROM   transaction
WHERE  amount + 3000 < 5000;
```

Use:

```
SELECT account_name, trans_date, amount
FROM   transaction
WHERE  amount < 2000;
```

In the following example, indexes will not be used when a column or columns appears on both sides of an operator. The result will be a full table scan.

Do not use:

```
SELECT account_name, trans_date, amount
FROM  transaction
WHERE account_name = NVL(:acc_name, account_name);
```

Use:

```
SELECT account_name, trans_date, amount
FROM  transaction
WHERE account_name LIKE NVL(:acc_name, '%');
```

As mentioned previously, function indexes can be used if the function in the WHERE clause represents the same function and column on which the function index was created. For function indexes to work, you must have the INIT.ORA parameter QUERY_REWRITE_ENABLED set to TRUE. You must also be using the cost-based analyzer. The statement in the following example uses a function index:

```
CREATE INDEX results_fn_ndx1 ON results(UPPER(owner))

SELECT count(*)
  FROM results
 WHERE UPPER(owner) = 'MR M A GURRY';

Execution Plan
-------------------------------------------
   0          SELECT STATEMENT Optimizer=CHOOSE (Cost=1
                     Card=1 Bytes=32)
   1    0     SORT (AGGREGATE)
   2    1       INDEX (RANGE SCAN) OF
               'RESULTS_FN_NDX1' (NON-UNIQUE)
               (Cost=1 Card=1 Bytes=32)
```

Another common problem that causes indexes not to be used is when the column indexed is one datatype and the value in the WHERE clause is another data type. Oracle automatically performs a simple column type conversion, or *casting*, when it compares two columns of different types. Assume that EMP_TYPE is an indexed VARCHAR2 column:

```
SELECT . . .
FROM   emp
WHERE  emp_type = 123

Execution Plan
-------------------------------------------
SELECT STATEMENT   OPTIMIZER HINT: CHOOSE
   TABLE ACCESS (FULL) OF 'EMP'
```

Because EMP_TYPE is a VARCHAR2 value, and the constant 123 is a numeric constant, Oracle will cast the VARCHAR2 value to a NUMBER value. This statement will actually be processed as:

```
SELECT . . .
FROM    emp
WHERE   TO_NUMBER(emp_type) = 123
```

The EXPLAIN PLAN utility cannot detect or identify casting problems; it simply assumes that all module bind variables are of the correct type. Programs that are not performing up to expectation may have a casting problem. The EXPLAIN PLAN output will report that the SQL statement is correctly using the index, but that won't necessarily be true.

Problem 2: Indexes Are Missing or Inappropriate

While it is important to use indexes to reduce response time, the use of indexes can often actually *lengthen* response times considerably. The problem occurs when more than 10% of a table's rows are accessed using an index.

I am astounded at how many tuners, albeit inexperienced, believe that if a SQL statement uses an index, it must be tuned. You should always ask, "Is it the best available index?", or "Could an additional index be added to improve the responsiveness?", or "Would a full table scan produce the result faster?"

Another important aspect of indexes is that depending on their type and composition, an index can affect the execution plan of a SQL statement. This must be considered when adding or modifying indexes.

Indexing versus full table scans

Figure 2 depicts why an index may cause more physical reads than performing a FULL TABLE SCAN on an index. The table on the left side in Figure 2 shows the index entries with the corresponding physical addresses on disk. The lines with the arrows depict physical reads from disk. Notice that each row accessed has a separate read.

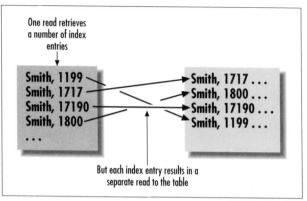

One read retrieves a number of index entries

Smith, 1199
Smith, 1717
Smith, 17190
Smith, 1800
...

Smith, 1717 ...
Smith, 1800 ...
Smith, 17190 ...
Smith, 1199 ...

But each index entry results in a separate read to the table

Figure 2. Physical reads caused by an index

A full table scan is typically able to read over 100 rows of table information per block. Added to this, the DB_FILE_MULTIBLOCK_READ_COUNT parameter allows Oracle to read many blocks with one physical disk read. You may be reading 800 rows with each physical read from disk. In comparison, an index will potentially perform one physical read for each row returned from the table.

If an index lookup is retrieving more than 10% of the rows in a table, the full table scan is likely to be a lot faster than index lookups followed by the additional physical reads to the table to retrieve the required data.

The exception to this rule is if the entire query can be satisfied by the index without the need to go to the table. In this case, an index lookup can be extremely effective. And if the SQL statement has an ORDER BY clause, and the index is ordered in the same order as the columns in the ORDER BY clause, a sort can be avoided, which can further improve performance.

Adding columns to indexes

In the following example, the runtime on the statement was reduced at a large stock brokerage from 40 seconds down to 3 seconds for account_id 100101, which happened to be the largest account in the table. The response time was critical for answering online customer inquiries. The problem was solved by adding all of the columns in the WHERE clause, and those in the SELECT list, into the index. There is the tradeoff that this index now has to be maintained, but the benefits at this site far outweighed the costs.

```
SELECT SUM(val)
    FROM        account_tran
    WHERE       account_id      = 100101
    AND     fin_yr              = '1996'
```

The original index was on (account_id). The new index was on (account_id, fin_yr, val). The result was that the index entirely satisfied the query, and the table did not need to be accessed.

Another common problem I notice is that when tables are joined, the leading column of the index is not the column(s) that the tables are joined on. Consider the following example:

```
WHERE A.SURNAME = 'GURRY'
        AND A.ACCT_NO = T.ACCT_NO
        AND T.TRAN_DATE > '01-JUL-97'
        AND T.TRAN_TYPE = 'SALARY'
```

In this situation, many sites will have an index on SURNAME for the ACCT table, and an index on TRAN_DATE and TRAN_TYPE for the TRANS table. To speed the query significantly, it is best to add the ACCT_NO join column as the leading column of the TRANS index. What you really want to have are indexes such as the following:

```
Index ACCT by (SURNAME)
Index TRANS by (ACCT_NO, TRAN_DATE, TRAN_TYPE)
```

Should I index small tables?

Yet another common problem that I see is small tables that don't have any index at all. I quite often hear heated debates with one person saying that the index is not required because the table is small and the data will be stored in memory anyway. They will often explain that the table can even be created with the cache attribute.

My experience has been that every small table should be indexed. The two reasons for the index are that the uniqueness of the rows in the table can be enforced by a primary or unique key, and, more importantly, the optimizer has the opportunity to work out the optimal execution plan for queries against the table. The example in the following table shows that the response time of a particular query went from 347 seconds elapsed down to 39.72 seconds elapsed when an index was created on the table. The most important thing about not having the index is that the optimizer will often create a less than optimal execution plan without it.

	Without index		With index	
	CPU	**Elapsed**	**CPU**	**Elapsed**
PARSE	0.00	0.03	0.01	0.11
EXECUTE	146.14	347.36	18.09	39.60
FETCH	0.00	0.00	0.00	0.00
TOTALS	146.14	347.39	18.10	39.72

Problem 3: Use of Single-Column Index Merge

Early in this reference, I mentioned that Oracle will only join single-column indexes. That is, unless you use the INDEX_JOIN hint. Single-column index merges are bad news in all relational databases, not just Oracle. They cause each index entry to be read for the designated value on both indexes.

Consider the following example, which is based on a schema used by a well-known stock brokerage:

```
INDEX1(APPROVE_FLAG) column and
INDEX2(ADVISOR_CODE)

SELECT COUNT(*)
  FROM account_master
    WHERE approve_flag='Y'
      AND  adviser_code='IAM';
```

3.509 secs

The number of ACCOUNT_MASTER rows that have APPROVE_FLAG = 'Y' is around one million. Oracle reads all of the Y's, and then reads the much lower number of ADIVISOR_CODE = 'IAM' rows, then crunches the results together. By the way, there is a much lower number of N's.

The good news is that Oracle has an easy way around this problem: simply create an index that contains both columns. In the example shown next, you would usually drop the single column index on ADVISOR_CODE after the new index is created:

```
CREATE INDEX mg1
ON account_master (adviser_code,
                   approve_flag)

SELECT COUNT(*)
  FROM account_master
    WHERE approve_flag='Y'
      AND  adviser_code='IAM';
```

0.041 secs

Note the improvement in execution time, from 3.509 seconds down to only 0.041 seconds.

Problem 4: Misuse of Nested Loop, Sort Merge, or Hash Join

If you leave all of the Oracle INIT.ORA parameters intact, there is a definite bias towards using nested loops for table joins. Nested loops are great for online transaction processing systems, but can be disastrous for reporting and batch processing systems. The rule-based optimizer will always use a nested loop unless prompted to use other methods by hints, or by other means such as dropping all indexes off the tables.

Online screens should definitely use nested loops, because data will be returned immediately. Typically a screen will buffer 20 rows and stop retrieving until the user requests the next set of data. If effective indexes are in place, a typical response time for getting a set of data will be a second or so.

As a rule of thumb, if a query returns less than 10% of the rows from the tables involved, you should be using nested loops. Use hash joins or sort merges if 10% or more of the rows are being returned.

To perform a hash join, a hash table is created in the memory of the smallest table, and then the other table is scanned. The rows from the second table are compared to the hash.

A hash join will usually run faster than a merge join (involving a sort, then a merge) if memory is adequate to hold the entire table that is being hashed. The entire result set must be determined before a single row is returned to the user. Therefore, hash joins are usually used for reporting and batch processing.

Many DBAs and developers blindly believe that a hash join is faster than a merge join. This is not always the case. For starters, a hash join can only be used for joins based on equality (=), and not for joins based on ranges (<, <=, >, >=). If I have a WHERE clause on the join columns such as WHERE o.owner <= w.owner, a hash join will *not* work.

Merge joins will work effectively for joins based on equality as well as for those based on ranges. In addition, merge joins will often run faster when all of the columns in the WHERE clause are pre-sorted by being in an index. In this case, the rows are simply plucked from the tables using the ROWID in the index.

With a merge join, all tables are sorted, unless all of the columns in the WHERE clause are contained within an index. This sort can be expensive, and it explains why a hash join will often run faster than a merge join. As with a hash join, the entire result set must be determined before a single row is returned to the user. Therefore, merge and hash joins are usually used for reporting and batch processing.

It is great to identify that we are using a nested loop when we shouldn't be, but what can we do about it? The answer is that you can consider using hints such as USE_NL, USE_HASH, or USE_MERGE. Hints are fine, but what if you are running packaged software and can't use hints? Perhaps you can create a view for reporting purposes, and place hints in the view. If you are running the rule-based optimizer, you can change to the cost-based optimizer. The cost-based optimizer has the intelligence to work out which join method is the best to use in a given situation.

Oracle also has several INIT.ORA parameters that affect the selection of nested loops, hash joins, and sort merges. The se parameters include SORT_AREA_SIZE, HASH_AREA_SIZE, HASH_JOIN_ENABLED, OPTIMIZER_MODE, DB_FILE_MULTIBLOCK_READ_COUNT, OPTIMIZER_MODE_ENABLE, OPTIMIZER_INDEX_CACHING, and OPTIMIZER_INDEX_COST_ADJ. All these parameters are described earlier, in the list in the section "Problem 6: Incorrect INIT.ORA Parameter Settings."

As an example of the impact of some of these parameters, I found that if the SORT_AREA_SIZE is left at its default and the HASH_AREA_SIZE is left at its default (which is twice the SORT_AREA_SIZE) the settings are 64K and 128K, respectively. I have tuned Oracle databases where the cost-based optimizer will simply not use hash joins unless the HASH_AREA_SIZE is over one megabyte.

Make sure that you are totally aware of the meaning of all the INIT.ORA parameters listed and their impact on the optimizer decision making.

Problem 5: Misuse of IN, EXISTS, NOT IN, NOT EXISTS, or Table Joins

You are probably wondering which is faster, NOT IN or NOT EXISTS. Should you choose IN, EXISTS, or a table join? The fact is that each can be faster than the other under certain circumstances. Even the dreaded NOT IN can be made to run fast with an appropriate hint inserted. This section lists examples from real-life sites that may assist you in determining which construct is best for a given situation.

When a join outperforms a subquery

As a general rule, table joins perform better than subqueries. My experience also suggests that, if you are forced to use a subquery, EXISTS outperforms IN in the majority of cases. However, there are always exceptions to the rule. The reason joins often run better than subqueries is that subqueries can result in full table scans, while joins are more likely to use indexes.

Consider the following example:

```
SELECT ..... FROM     emp  e
WHERE        EXISTS
    (SELECT 'x'
    FROM dept d
    WHERE d.dept_no = e.dept_no
    AND d.dept_cat = 'FIN');

real: 47578

0    SELECT STATEMENT Optimizer=CHOOSE
1    0    SORT (AGGREGATE)
2    1      FILTER
3    2 TABLE ACCESS (FULL) OF 'EMP'
4    2        AND-EQUAL
```

```
5   4    INDEX (RANGE SCAN) OF 'DEPT_NDX1'
             (NON-UNIQUE)
6   4    INDEX (RANGE SCAN) OF
             'DEPT_NDX2' (NON-UNIQUE)
```

Note the full table scan on EMP; also note the 47,578 milli-seconds of elapsed time required to execute the statement. Joins are more likely to use indexes. The following query, which returns the same result, executes much faster:

```
SELECT  .... FROM  emp e, dept d
WHERE   e.dept_no = d.dept_no
AND     d.dept_cat = 'FIN';

    real: 2153


0   SELECT STATEMENT Optimizer=CHOOSE
1   0    SORT (AGGREGATE)
2   1      NESTED LOOPS
3   2        TABLE ACCESS (BY ROWID) OF 'DEPT'
4   3          INDEX (RANGE SCAN) OF 'DEPT_NDX2'
                 (NON-UNIQUE)
5   2        INDEX (RANGE SCAN) OF 'EMP_NDX1'
               (NON-UNIQUE)
```

As you can see, the query using a join executed in only 2,153 milliseconds as opposed to the 47,578 milliseconds required when a subquery was used.

Which is faster, IN or EXISTS?

The answer is that either can be faster depending on the cir-cumstance. If EXISTS is used, the execution path is driven by the tables in the outer select; if IN is used, the subquery is evaluated first, and then joined to each row returned by the outer query.

In the following example, notice that the HORSES table from the outer SELECT is processed first, and it drives the query:

```
SELECT h.horse_name
  FROM horses h
 WHERE horse_name like 'C%'
```

```
   AND exists
   (SELECT 'x'
      FROM WINNERS  w
    WHERE w.position = 1
      AND w.location = 'MOONEE VALLEY'
      AND h.horse_name  = w.horse_name)
Execution Plan
-------------------------------------------
   0     SELECT STATEMENT Optimizer=CHOOSE
   1     0   FILTER
   1     1   INDEX (RANGE SCAN) OF
   2     'HORSES_PK' (UNIQUE)
   3     1 TABLE ACCESS (BY INDEX
   4         ROWID) OF 'WINNERS'
   5     3 INDEX (RANGE SCAN) OF
   6       'WINNERS_NDX1' (NON-UNIQUE)
```

The situation is reversed when IN is used. The following
query produces identical results, but uses IN instead of
EXISTS. Notice that the table in the subquery is accessed
first, and that drives the query:

```
SELECT h.horse_name
  FROM horses h
 WHERE horse_name like 'C%'
   AND horse_name IN
   (SELECT horse_name
      FROM WINNERS  w
    WHERE w.position = 1
      AND w.location = 'MOONEE VALLEY')

Execution Plan
-------------------------------------------
   0      SELECT STATEMENT Optimizer=CHOOSE
   1    0    NESTED LOOPS
   2    1      VIEW OF 'VW_NSO_1'
   3    2        SORT (UNIQUE)
   4    3        TABLE ACCESS (BY INDEX
                   ROWID) OF 'WINNERS'
   5    4          INDEX (RANGE SCAN) OF
                     'WINNERS_NDX4' (NON-UNIQUE)
   6    1      INDEX (UNIQUE SCAN) OF
                   'HORSES_PK' (UNIQUE)
```

It is fair to say that in most cases, it is best to use the EXISTS
rather than the IN. The exception is when a very small

number of rows exist in the table in the subquery, and the table in the main query has a large number of rows that are required to be read to satisfy the query.

The following example uses a temporary table that typically has only 2,000 rows. The table is used in the subquery. The outer table has over 16,000,000 rows. In this example, the subquery is being joined to the main table using all of the primary key columns in the main table. This is an example of IN running considerably faster than the EXISTS.

First the EXISTS-based solution:

```
DELETE FROM
  FROM ps_pf_ledger_f00
 WHERE EXISTS
(SELECT 'x'
FROM ps_pf_led_pst2_t1 b
WHERE b.business_unit    = ps_pf_ledger_f00.business_unit
AND b.fiscal_year        = ps_pf_ledger_f00.fiscal_year
AND b.accounting_period= ps_pf_ledger_f00.accounting_
period
AND b.pf_scenario_id = ps_pf_ledger_f00.pf_scenario_id
AND b.source             = ps_pf_ledger_f00.source
AND b.account            = ps_pf_ledger_f00.account
AND b.deptid             = ps_pf_ledger_f00.deptid
AND b.cust_id            = ps_pf_ledger_f00.cust_id
AND b.product_id         = ps_pf_ledger_f00.product_id
AND b.channel_id         = ps_pf_ledger_f00.channel_id
AND b.obj_id             = ps_pf_ledger_f00.obj_id
AND b.currency_cd        = ps_pf_ledger_f00.currency_cd);
```

Elapsed: 00:08:160.51

Notice the elapsed time. Next is the IN-based version of the same query. Notice the greatly reduced elapsed execution time:

```
DELETE FROM ps_pf_ledger_f00
WHERE( business_unit,fiscal_year,accounting_period,
       pf_scenario_id ,account,deptid ,cust_id ,
       product_id,channel_id,obj_id,currency_cd)
IN
(SELECT business_unit,fiscal_year,accounting_period,
        pf_scenario_id ,account,deptid ,cust_id ,
```

```
          product_id,channel_id,obj_id,currency_cd
    FROM ps_pf_led_pst2_t1 );
```

Elapsed: 00:00:00.30

To help speed up EXISTS processing, you can often utilize
the HASH_SJ and MERGE_SJ hints (both are described in
detail in "Using SQL Hints," later in this book). These hints
allow Oracle to return the rows in the subquery only once.
For example:

```
UPDATE PS_JRNL_LN
SET JRNL_LINE_STATUS = 'D'
WHERE BUSINESS_UNIT = 'A023'
AND PROCESS_INSTANCE=0001070341
AND JOURNAL_DATE
 IN ( TO_DATE('2001-08-01','YYYY-MM-DD'),
      TO_DATE('2001-08-14','YYYY-MM-DD'))
AND LEDGER IN ( 'ACTUALS')
AND JRNL_LINE_STATUS = '0'
AND EXISTS
(SELECT /*+ HASH_SJ */ 'X'
FROM  PS_COMBO_DATA_TBL
WHERE SETID='AMP'
  AND PROCESS_GROUP='SERVICE01'
  AND COMBINATION IN ('SERVICE01',
       'SERVICE02', 'STAT_SERV1')
  AND VALID_CODE='V'
  AND PS_JRNL_LN.JOURNAL_DATE BETWEEN
          EFFDT_FROM AND EFFDT_TO
  AND PS_JRNL_LN.ACCOUNT = ACCOUNT
  AND PS_JRNL_LN.DEPTID = DEPTID)

UPDATE STATEMENT Optimizer=CHOOSE (Cost=9 Card=1 Bytes=80)
  UPDATE OF PS_JRNL_LN
    HASH JOIN (SEMI) (Cost=9 Card=1
                      Bytes=80)
      TABLE ACCESS (BY INDEX ROWID) OF
        PS_JRNL_LN (Cost=4 Card=1
                   Bytes=33)
        INDEX (RANGE SCAN) OF PSDJRNL_LN
          (NON-UNIQUE) (Cost=3 Card=1)
      INLIST ITERATOR
        TABLE ACCESS (BY INDEX ROWID) OF
          PS_COMBO_DATA_TBL (Cost=4
            Card=12 Bytes=564)
```

```
    INDEX (RANGE SCAN) OF
    PSACOMBO_DATA_TBL (NON-UNIQUE)
      (Cost=3 Card=12)
```

The Peoplesoft example shown was running for two hours without the HASH_SJ and reduced to an incredible four minutes with the hint. The hint forces the subquery SELECT rows to be read only once and then joined to the table outside the subquery (PS_JRNL_LN). The same effect can be obtained by setting the INIT.ORA parameter ALWAYS_SEMI_JOIN=HASH.

Problem 6: Unnecessary Sorts

Despite a multitude of improvements in the way that Oracle handles sorts, including bypassing the buffer cache, having tablespaces especially set up as type temporary, and using memory more effectively, operations that include sorts can be expensive and should be avoided where practical.

The operations that require a sort include the following:

CREATE INDEX
DISTINCT
GROUP BY
ORDER BY
INTERSECT
MINUS
UNIONS
UNINDEXED TABLE JOINS

There are many things a DBA can do to improve sorting, such as making sure that the sorting tablespace is a TEMPORARY tablespace, having a large SORT_AREA_SIZE to allow more sorts to occur in memory, ensuring that the default INITIAL and NEXT extents on the TEMP tablespace are a multiple of the SORT_AREA_SIZE parameter, and ensuring that all users are correctly assigned to the TEMP tablespace for their sorting.

There are also things that you can do in your SQL to avoid sorts, discussed in the following sections.

Consider UNION ALL in place of UNION

Programmers of complex query statements that include a UNION clause should always ask whether a UNION ALL will suffice. The UNION clause forces all rows returned by the different queries in the UNION to be sorted and merged in order to filter out duplicates before the first row can be returned to the calling module. A UNION ALL simply returns *all* rows, including duplicates, and does not have to perform any sort, merge, or filtering operations.

Consider the following UNION query:

```
SELECT acct_num, balance_amt
FROM   debit_transactions
WHERE  tran_date = '31-DEC-95'
UNION
SELECT acct_num, balance_amt
FROM   credit_transactions
WHERE  tran_date = '31-DEC-95'
```

To improve performance, replace this code with the following UNION ALL query:

```
SELECT acct_num, balance_amt
FROM   debit_transactions
WHERE  tran_date = '31-DEC-95'
UNION ALL
SELECT acct_num, balance_amt
FROM   credit_transactions
WHERE  tran_date = '31-DEC-95'
```

Of course, if your program depends on duplicate rows being eliminated by the database, you have no choice but to use UNION.

Consider using an index to avoid a sort

Indexes can be used to avoid the need to perform sorts. Indexes are stored in ascending order by default. If the columns in your ORDER BY clause are in the same sequence as

---

the columns in an index, forcing the statement to use that index will cause the data to be returned in the desired order.

To force the usage of the index, you can either add a hint or use a dummy WHERE clause. Consider the following statement that executes against a table having an index on (ACC_NAME, ACC_SURNAME):

```
SELECT acc_name, acc_surname
FROM account acct
ORDER BY acc_name
```

The following version of this statement uses a hint to force use of an index:

```
SELECT /*+ INDEX_ASC(acct acc_ndx1) */ acc_name,
    acc_surname
FROM account acct
ORDER BY acc_name
```

A dummy WHERE clause, on the other hand, is often placed onto online inquiry screens. The following example uses WHERE acc_name > chr(1) in place of the ORDER BY clause. The WHERE clause forces the use of the index, which results in rows being returned in sorted order. One advantage of eliminating the sort in an online application is that the first screenful of rows can be returned quickly.

```
SELECT acc_name, acc_surname
    FROM account
WHERE acc_name > chr(1)
```

In a statement like this, there is no need to have the ORDER BY clause. If the ORDER BY clause was specified, and the user put in a BLANK for his selection and pressed the GO button, every single row in the table would need to be sorted before a single row could be returned. This could take a considerable amount of time, and is not desirable behavior in an OLTP environment.

Problem 7: Too Many Indexes on a Table

I've visited sites that have a standard in place saying that no table can have more than six indexes. This will often cause almost all SQL statements to run beautifully, but a handful of statements to run badly, and indexes can't be added because there are already six on the table.

Sometimes indexes may be redundant, such as an INDEX_1 on (A, B), INDEX_2 on (A, B, C), and INDEX_3 on (A, B, C, D). In such cases, DBAs often suggest dropping the first two indexes because they are redundant; i.e., they have the same leading columns, in the same order, as INDEX_3. Dropping redundant indexes, however, may cause problems with the selection of a new driving table on a join using the rule-based optimizer (see the "What the RBO rules don't tell you" sections earlier in this book). There is far less risk associated with dropping redundant indexes when the cost-based optimizer is being utilized.

Having lots of indexes on a table will usually have only a small impact on OLTP systems, because only a few rows are processed in a single transaction, and the impact of updating many indexes is only milliseconds.

Having lots of indexes can be extremely harmful for batch update processing, with its typically high number of inserts, updates, and deletes. Table 5 demonstrates this.

Table 5. Impact of multiple indexes on insert performance

Number of inserts and indexes	Runtime
Inserting 256 rows with 0 indexes	1.101 seconds
Inserting 512 rows with 0 indexes	1.161 seconds
Inserting 256 rows with 5 indexes	3.936 seconds
Inserting 512 rows with 5 indexes	12.788 seconds
Inserting 256 rows with 10 indexes	12.558 seconds
Inserting 512 rows with 10 indexes	22.132 seconds

Some sites overcome the problem of having many indexes on a table by dropping all indexes prior to batch updates, and re-creating them after the batch run is complete. Oracle has added lots of functionality to help speed index rebuilds. For example, you can rebuild indexes with the NOLOGGING or UNRECOVERABLE options, and you can rebuild indexes in parallel. Despite these enhancements, tables may get to a size at which the index rebuild process takes longer than running a batch update with the indexes intact.

My recommendation is to avoid rules stating that a site will not have any more than a certain number of indexes.

Oracle9*i* adds some great new functionality that allows you to identify indexes that are not being used. The command is ALTER INDEX MONITORING USAGE. Take advantage of it to identify and remove unused indexes.

The bottom line is that all SQL statements must run acceptably. There is ALWAYS a way of achieving this. If it requires having 10 indexes on a table, then you should put 10 indexes on the table.

Problem 8: Use of OR Instead of UNION

When we visit sites to tune SQL, we always seem to identify a few unusual problems that are easily remedied. The OR EXISTS subquery is just such a headache. We have found statements similar to the following at several sites:

```
select     .....
 from   ps_jrnl_header a
where   jrnl_hdr_status ='E'
or exists
 (select   'x'
    from  ps_jrnl_header
   where business_unit_iu=a.business_unit_iu
     and journal_id= a.journal_id
     and journal_date=a.journal_date
     and unpost_seq=  a.unpost_seq
     and jrnl_hdr_status='E')
```

Runtime: 4 Minute 16 seconds

Notice the long runtime for the statement. Wouldn't it be nice to make the statement go faster? Luckily, the fix is simple. If you have access to change the code (i.e., you are not

running a third-party package), use a UNION statement to
implement the OR in the WHERE clause as two separate
queries:

```
select              ...........
from                ps_jrnl_header a
where               jrnl_hdr_status ='E'
UNION
select              .....
from                       ps_jrnl_header     a, ps_jrnl_
header b
where                      b.business_unit_iu
            =a.business_unit_iu
    and                    b.journal_id=a.journal_id
    and                    b.journal_date=a.journal_date
    and                    b.unpost_seq=a.unpost_seq
    and                    a.jrnl_hdr_status='E'
    and                    b.jrnl_hdr_status != 'E';
```

Runtime: 0.02 seconds

The reason for the performance improvement is that the
UNION allows the optimizer to perform two simple operations to return the rows, whereas the more complex OR construct has confused the optimizer into using a less optimal
execution plan.

Problem 9: Tables and Indexes with Many Deletes

Oracle is similar to many other databases in that there are
performance issues with deletes. Oracle has a high water
mark, which represents the highest number of rows ever
inserted into the table. This high-water mark can have an
impact on performance. Consider the following example,
which takes 5.378 seconds to read a table with 151,070 rows:

```
SELECT COUNT(*) FROM YYYY;
151070

real: 5378
```

It just happens that all 150,000 rows have the STATE column set to 'VIC', and that the table has an index on the STATE column. If I use a WHERE clause to force the count to use the index on the STATE, it takes 16.884 seconds:

```
SELECT COUNT(*) FROM YYYY  WHERE  STATE='VIC';
---------
    151070

real: 16884
```

Notice that the index scan took about three times longer than the full table scan. By the way, this SELECT statement was done using the rule-based optimizer. The cost-based optimizer would have performed a full table scan.

Now let's delete all of the rows, so that the result is an empty table:

```
DELETE FROM YYYY;

real: 55277
```

Now that we have an empty table, let's count all the rows again:

```
SELECT COUNT(*) FROM YYYY;
---------
        0

real: 5117
```

Notice that it takes the same amount of time to count zero rows as it took to count from the table when it was completely populated. This is because, when performing a full table scan, Oracle reads as far as the table's high-water mark, and the high-water mark has not changed.

Let's count the rows again using the index:

```
. SELECT COUNT(*) FROM YYYY  WHERE STATE='VIC';
   0
   real: 16029
```

Just as before, it takes the same amount of time to count zero rows as it took to count the original 150,000. This is because

---

the index entries are logically deleted, but still exist physically.

The table has never had any rows with a state equal to 'NSW' (New South Wales), so let's try counting the 'NSW' rows:

```
SELECT COUNT(*) FROM YYYY WHERE STATE='NSW';
real: 16940
```

The count still takes the same amount time as before, when counting the 'VIC' rows. This is because scanning the index requires Oracle to scan past the logically deleted Victorian ('VIC') entries.

To avoid the types of performance problems I've just demonstrated, my recommendation is to rebuild a table, and its indexes, whenever the table has undergone many deletes. If index columns are frequently updated, you should also rebuild the indexes, because an update forces a logical delete in the index followed by an insert of the new, updated entry. Some sites go as far as rebuilding indexes nightly when they have a lot of logical delete activity.

To detect which tables have many deletes and updates, you can run the following SELECT statement:

```
SELECT sql_text, executions
   FROM v$sqlarea
 WHERE UPPER(sql_text) LIKE 'DELETE%'
                    OR
       UPPER(sql_text) LIKE 'UPDATE%';
```

The output from this statement will contain SQL statements on tables that have many deletes and updates. You should consider regular rebuilds of indexes on these tables.

Other Problems: Heavy Usage of Views

Another common problem I see is heavy usage of views of views, which can totally confuse both optimizers as well as the person trying to work out how to tune the resulting monstrosity. Keep in mind that using hints in views of views will often not give consistent and good performance. Using hints on the outer view is preferable to using hints on the inner view.

Other Problems: Joining Too Many Tables

Joining more than five tables will almost always confuse both optimizers, and produce a poor execution plan. See "Problem 5: Joining Too Many Tables" under "Cost-Based Optimizer Problems and Solutions." If you are lucky enough to be able to change the SQL to use hints, you can overcome the problem.

Joining more than five tables frequently in an application usually points to not enough performance consideration at the design stage, when the logical data model was translated into a physical data model.

Handy SQL Tuning Tips

The following sections list some SQL tuning tips that you may find useful both when writing SQL statements and when troubleshooting performance problems.

Identify Bad SQL

The SQL statements in this section demonstrate how to identify SQL statements that have an expected response time of more than 10 seconds. The assumption has been made that 300 disk I/Os can be performed per second, and that 4,000 buffer gets can be performed per second. These times are typical of a medium- to high-end machine.

Use the following SQL*Plus commands to identify statements using, on average, more than 3,000 disk reads (10 seconds' worth) per execution:

```
column "Response" format 999,999,999.99;
column nl newline;
```

```
ttitle 'SQL With Disk Reads > 10 Seconds'

SELECT sql_text nl, 'Executions='||
            executions  nl,
   'Expected Response Time in Seconds= ',
    disk_reads / decode(executions, 0, 1,
                       executions) / 300
               "Response"
   FROM v$sql
 WHERE  disk_reads / decode(executions,0,1, executions)
                     / 300 > 10
   AND executions > 0
ORDER BY hash_value, child_number;
```

Similarly, the following SQL*Plus commands identify statements that result in more than 40,000 buffer gets:

```
column "Response" format 999,999,999.99
ttitle 'SQL Buffer Scan > 10 Seconds'

SELECT sql_text nl, 'Executions='||
    executions  nl,
    'Expected Response Time in Seconds= ',
    buffer_gets /
      decode(executions, 0, 1, executions)
                / 4000 "Response"
   FROM v$sql
  WHERE  buffer_gets /
      decode(executions, 0,1, executions)
                     /   4000 > 10
    AND executions > 0
ORDER BY hash_value, child_number;
```

Once you've identified poorly performing SQL statements, you can work to tune them.

Identify Long-Running SQL Statements

Oracle8*i* and later has a great feature that stores information on long-running queries currently active in the V$SESSION_ LONGOPS view.

The following example shows the results of a query against V$SESSION_LONGOPS:

```
SELECT username, sql_text, sofar, totalwork, units
  FROM v$sql, v$session_longops
 WHERE sql_address=address
   AND sql_hash_value=hash_value
 ORDER BY address, hash_value, child_number

HROA
select count(*) from winners w1, winners_backup w2 where
w1.owner=w2.owner||''
       1061       7098 Blocks
```

In this example, the HROA user is running a SELECT COUNT that is about 15% complete. In other words, it has processed 1,061 blocks out of 7,098 (1061/7098 = 15%). The statement has been written to not use an index on the OWNER column of the WINNERS_BACKUP table, because it has a concatenation against that column. Perhaps the DBA should phone the HROA user and question the statement, maybe even canceling it if it is going to run for much longer.

Use DECODE for IF/ELSE Selection

Programmers often need a way to count and/or add up variable conditions for a group of rows. The DECODE statement provides a very efficient way of doing this. Because DECODE is rather complex, few programmers take the time to learn to use this statement to full advantage. The following statement uses DECODE to count the number of first, second, and third placings a racehorse has run:

```
SELECT horse_name, to_char(sum(decode(position,1,1,0)))
     , to_char(sum(decode(position,2,1,0)))
     , to_char(sum(decode(position,3,1,0)))
  FROM winners
 GROUP BY horse_name
```

In the sum(decode(position,2,1,0)) construct, we are saying that if the horse's finishing position is 2 (second), add one to the count of seconds. The results of this statement appear as follows:

Horse	Firsts	Seconds	Thirds
Wild Charm	1	2	2

The alternative statement without the decode involves scanning the table three times, rather than once, as in the previous statement.

```
SELECT horse_name
     , count(w1.position)
     , count(w2.position)
     , count(w3.position)
  FROM winners w1, winners w2, winners w3
 WHERE w1.horse_name = w2.horse_name
   AND w2.horse_name = w3.horse_name
   AND w1.position   = 1
   AND w2.position   = 2
   AND w3.position   = 3
 GROUP BY horse_name
```

Encourage Bind Variables

The values of bind variables do not need to be the same for two statements to be considered identical. If the bind variable references are the same, the parsed forms of the statements are considered to be the same. Consequently, the statements share the same parsed form in the shared pool area in memory.

Following are two sharable SQL statements:

```
SELECT * FROM emp WHERE emp_no = :B1;   Bind value: 123
SELECT * FROM emp WHERE emp_no = :B1;   Bind value: 987
```

These statements are shareable because bind variables have been used, making the statements themselves identical. The actual bind values do not result in one statement being different from the other.

Following are two non-sharable SQL statements. These statements are not sharable because bind variables have not been used, and the resulting hardcoded values make the statements different from each other.

```
SELECT * FROM emp WHERE emp_no = 123;
SELECT * FROM emp WHERE emp_no = 987;
```

In general, encourage your programmers to use bind variables in favor of hardcoding variable values. This will allow their statements to be stored once in memory rather than once for each distinct combination of variable values. Coding bind variables may mean extra effort, and should be attempted only when you are sure that a particular SQL statement will be used repetitively, with the only difference being bind variable values.

There is one situation in which bind variables are not such a great choice. If you have column data in a table having a disproportionate number of rows with certain values, and a very small number of rows with other values, you should be using histograms. Bind variables cannot use histogram information.

Imagine that you have a three-million row ACCOUNT table that has a SUSPENSE account with one million rows. All other accounts in the table have an average of a few hundred rows each. It is most efficient to do a full table scan when a user specifies WHERE ACCOUNT='SUSPENSE' in a WHERE clause. On the other hand, it is far more efficient to use an index on the ACCOUNT column if any other account type is selected.

The cost-based optimizer can use histograms to intelligently utilize either the full table scan or the index scan where appropriate, based on the value specified in the WHERE clause. Using bind variables will prevent the optimizer from doing this, because the optimizer is unaware of the value that will be in the bind variable at the time it decides on the execution plan.

Oracle8*i* introduced a parameter named CURSOR_SHARING. This parameter allows you to hardcode your WHERE values with literals, numbers, or dates and still have them be shared, and stored only once in memory. This applies if you have the CURSOR_SHARING parameter set to FORCE or SIMILAR. Using this parameter, and hardcoding values in your WHERE clauses, will assist the cost-based optimizer in making substantially better decisions.

Beginning with Oracle9*i*, the optimizer will consider bind variable values when choosing execution plans. This avoids having to hardcode values and rely on CURSOR_SHARING = FORCE or SIMILAR to obtain the advantages of bind variables.

Using SQL Hints

Hints can be placed into your SQL statements to force the optimizers to utilize a particular execution path for absolute best performance. The following sections describe available hints up through Oracle9*i*.

By including your own optimization hints as "comments" within the SQL statement, you force the statement to follow your desired retrieval path, rather than the one calculated by the optimizer. In the following example, including /*+ RULE */ inside the SELECT statement instructs the optimizer to use the rule-based optimizer rather than the cost-based optimizer:

```
SELECT    /*+ RULE */  . . . .
   FROM    emp, dept
  WHERE    . . .
```

The optimizer hint(s) can be included only immediately after the initial SQL "action" verb and most are ignored when included in INSERT statements:

```
SELECT /*+ hint text */  . . . .
DELETE /*+ hint text */  . . . .
UPDATE /*+ hint text */  . . . .
```

Each hint is operational only within the *statement block* for which it appears. A statement block is one of the following:

- A simple SELECT, DELETE, or UPDATE statement
- The parent portion of a complex statement

- The subquery portion of a complex statement
- Part of a compound query

Consider these examples:

```
SELECT  /*+ RULE */  . . . .
FROM    emp
WHERE   emp_status = 'PART-TIME'
AND     EXISTS
    ( SELECT  /*+ FIRST_ROWS */  'x'
       FROM  emp_history
      WHERE   emp_no = E.emp_no
        AND   emp_status
            != 'PART-TIME' )

SELECT  /*+ RULE */  . . . .
FROM    emp
WHERE   emp_status = 'PART-TIME'
UNION
SELECT  /*+ ALL_ROWS */  . . . .
FROM    emp_history
WHERE   emp_status != 'PART-TIME'
```

When Are Hints Ignored?

The optimizer cannot distinguish a bad hint from a programmer comment. An incorrectly structured or misspelled hint will be ignored rather than reported as an error.

The following list covers some of the more common mistakes people make when programming with hints. The list does not include the obvious, such as misspelling the hint or object name.

Table aliases

All hints that require a TABLE parameter must correctly specify the table. This means that if the table is referenced via an alias within the SQL statement, the hint must also reference it via the alias. For example:

```
    SELECT /*+ INDEX(emp emp_PK) */ ...
FROM    emp E
    WHERE  E.emp_no = 12345
```

In this example, the hint will be ignored because it references a table named emp. The hint should reference E, because E is the alias given to the emp table.

Invalid hint location

Hints can appear only immediately after the first SQL verb of a statement block. If you position a hint anywhere else in the statement, it will be ignored. The following examples all illustrate correct hint placement:

```
SELECT  /*+ hint text */  . . . .
DELETE  /*+ hint text */  . . . .
UPDATE  /*+ hint text */  . . . .

SELECT  /*+ RULE */  . . . .
FROM    emp
WHERE   emp_status = 'PART-TIME'
UNION
SELECT  /*+ ALL_ROWS */  . . . .
FROM    emp_history
WHERE   emp_status != 'PART-TIME'
```

Using Hints in Views

Oracle discourages the usage of hints in views because views can be used in different contexts from one usage to the next. I agree that views can be used in different contexts, but I must state that hints in views are one of the most useful tuning mechanisms available. I have found hints in views particularly useful for end-user reporting. Some reporting products, such as Peoplesoft nVision, cannot run anywhere near their optimum without hints being applied.

Available Hints

The following is a list of all hints available in Oracle9i. Many of the hints are also available in earlier releases of Oracle. The purpose of this list is not to exhaustively describe the syntax of each hint, but to show the way each hint is most commonly used.

ALL_ROWS

Optimizes for least resource usage to return all rows required by the query. This hint will sometimes override a NESTED LOOP with a SORT MERGE or a HASH JOIN if applied to a SELECT, UPDATE, or DELETE statement when OPTIMIZER_MODE=CHOOSE.

```
SELECT /*+ ALL_ROWS */ ...
```

AND_EQUAL *(table index1 index2[... index5])*

Explicitly merges single-column indexes. A minimum of two indexes must be specified, and no more than five are allowed. Single-column index merges can be incredibly inefficient if the first index in the WHERE returns a lot of rows.

```
SELECT /*+ AND_EQUAL(horse_owners ho_ndx1
           ho_ndx2 ho_ndx3) */
       count(*)
  FROM horse_owners
 WHERE horse_name = 'WILD CHARM'
   AND owner      = 'Mr M A Gurry'
   AND identifier = 14;
```

APPEND

Allows a direct path insert to a table. Data to be inserted bypasses the buffer cache, and is appended to the end of the table. Integrity constraints are ignored during the load, although I have observed that after the load has taken place, the integrity checks are made and your statement can still fail with an integrity constraint error.

```
INSERT /*+ APPEND */ * INTO y
SELECT FROM winners;
```

CACHE *(table)*

Instructs the optimizer to position all blocks retrieved via a full table scan at the *most* recently used end of the LRU (Least Recently Used) list in the buffer cache. You would usually use this hint on small tables, but I have seen sites with a very large amount of memory cache very large tables that are infrequently changed.

```
SELECT /*+ FULL(winners) CACHE(winners)
       */ count(*)
  FROM winners
```

CHOOSE

Uses the cost-based optimizer if statistics are available for at least one table; otherwise, uses the rule-based optimizer.

```
SELECT /*+ CHOOSE */
```

CLUSTER(table)

Forces the use of a cluster scan for the specified table. This hint can only be used for objects that are clustered. A cluster is two or more related tables with the parents and the related child records stored physically next to each other. For example, account1 will have its transactions stored in the same physical block as the account record.

```
SELECT /*+ CLUSTER(a) */ acct_name
  FROM acct a
```

CURSOR_SHARING_EXACT

Prevents Oracle from translating literals into bind variables even when the CURSOR_SHARING parameter is set to FORCE or SIMILAR. For example:

```
SELECT /*+ CURSOR_SHARING_EXACT */ name, suburb
  FROM emp
 WHERE surname = 'GURRY';
```

If the hint was not used on this SQL statement, and CURSOR_SHARING was set to SIMILAR or FORCE, the 'GURRY' value in this example would be translated into a bind variable.

FACT(table)

Tells the cost-based optimizer that the table listed is a fact table and should be treated as such. This hint is used with the STAR_TRANSFORMATION operation.

```
SELECT /*+ FACT(results) */
```

FIRST_ROWS or FIRST_ROWS(n)

Optimizes for best response time to return the first *n* rows required by a query. Statistics do not have to be available for any table involved in the SQL statement; their statistics can be estimated by the optimizer. Other "access path hints" can be included with the FIRST_ROWS hint, and may override FIRST_ROWS. If you use the (n) option to specify the exact number of rows to be returned, Oracle can make a more precise execution plan decision. The (n) option is only available with Oracle9*i* and later.

For example:

```
SELECT /*+ FIRST_ROWS(100) */
```

This hint:

- Will always choose an index over a full table scan.
- Uses nested loop joins over sort/merge joins, where possible.
- Uses an index to satisfy an ORDER BY clause, where possible.

The optimizer ignores the hints for DELETE and UPDATE statement blocks, and for any SELECT statement block that contains a "grouping" operation (UNION, INTERSECT, MINUS, GROUP BY, DISTINCT, MAX, MIN, SUM, etc.) or a FOR UPDATE clause. Such statements cannot be optimized for best response time, because all rows must be accessed before the first row can be returned.

FULL(table)

Forces the use of a full table scan on the specified table.

```
SELECT /*+ FULL(emp) */  ename
  FROM emp
WHERE commencement_date > sysdate - 7
```

If a table has an alias, you must specify the alias name in the hint:

```
SELECT /*+ FULL(a) */  ename
  FROM emp a
WHERE a.commencement_date > sysdate - 7
```

HASH(table)

Forces the use of a hash table scan for the specified table. This hint applies only to tables stored in a cluster.

```
SELECT /*+ HASH(a) */ acct_name
  FROM acct a
```

A lot of people get this hint mixed up with USE_HASH, which forces a hash join. This is *not* the same hint!

HASH_AJ

Provides substantial performance improvements by turning a nested loop operation for a NOT IN into a hash join operation. This hint needs to be placed against the SELECT statement in the subquery, *not* in the main select clause.

```
SELECT count(*)
  FROM horses
WHERE horse_name LIKE 'M%'
  AND horse_name NOT IN
  ( SELECT /*+ HASH_AJ */ horse_name
      FROM horse_owners
     WHERE owner LIKE '%Lombardo%');
```

HASH_SJ

Often speeds response times in an EXISTS subquery by returning the rows in the subquery only once.

```
SELECT count(*)
  FROM horses
WHERE horse_name LIKE 'M%'
  AND EXISTS
  ( SELECT /*+ HASH_SJ */ horse_name
      FROM horse_owners
     WHERE owner LIKE '%Lombardo%'
       AND horses.horse_name= horse_owners.horse_name)
```

There are some restrictions on this hint:

a. There must be only one table listed in the subquery.

b. The hint can't be used in a subquery within a sub-query.

c. The subquery must be correlated with an equality predicate, which is a requirement for all hash joins.

d. The subquery must have no GROUP BY clause, CONNECT BY clause, or ROWNUM reference.

INDEX(table [index [index...]])

Forces the use of an indexed table scan for the specified table. You can optionally specify one or more indexes in the hint. If no indexes are included, the optimizer calculates the cost of all indexes for the table, and uses the most efficient (several indexes may be used in tandem). If several indexes are listed, the optimizer calculates the cost of only those indexes that are specified, and uses the most efficient (several indexes from the list may be used in tandem if they are single-column indexes). If a single index is specified, the optimizer performs a scan using that index.

```
SELECT /*+ INDEX(EMP EMP_NDX1) */
SELECT /*+ INDEX(EMP) */
```

INDEX_ASC(table [index])

Forces the use of an ascending indexed table scan for the specified table. Oracle will scan indexes in ascending order by default anyway. So why use this hint? Good question! I suppose this hint guarantees that the index will be traversed in ascending order, even if Oracle decides to behave differently. The exception to the rule is if the index has been created as a reverse key index, e.g., CREATE INDEX POST ON OWNERS (ZIPCODE) REVERSE.

```
SELECT /*+ INDEX_ASC(EMP EMP_NDX1) */...
```

INDEX_COMBINE(table [index [index...]])

Explicitly chooses bitmap indexes to access the table information.

```
SELECT /*+ INDEX_COMBINE(ACCT_TRAN AT_STATE_BMI AT_
TYPE_BMI) */
```

INDEX_DESC(table [index])

Forces the use of a descending indexed table scan for the specified table. By default, Oracle scans indexes in ascending sequence. This hint guarantees that the index will be traversed in descending order. A typical usage of this hint would be to retrieve the latest transactions on your bank account in descending order by date. This hint can be of great value in distributed queries.

```
SELECT /*+ INDEX_DESC(ACCT_TRANS ACCT_TRANS_DATE_NDX)
*/...
```

INDEX_FFS(table [index])

Instructs the optimizer to do a full scan of an index rather than a full scan of a table. The index scan can sometimes run faster, but if and only if every column in the WHERE clause for the specified table exists in the index.

```
SELECT /*+ INDEX_FFS(ACCT_TRAN AT_STATE_NDX1) */
```

INDEX_JOIN(table [index] table [index2])

This hint tells the optimizer to join two indexes as the access path. Typically the execution plan will include a hash join of the two indexes, which can return some performance improvements. In the following example, two of the table's three primary key columns have been used in the WHERE clause (HORSE_NAME and OWNER), as has the leading column (IDENTIFIER) of a non-primary key index.

```
SELECT /*+ INDEX_JOIN(HORSE_OWNERS  HO_NDX2 HO_PK) */
       Horse_name, owner
  FROM HORSE_OWNERS
 WHERE horse_name = 'WILD CHARM'
   AND owner = 'Mr M A Gurry'
   AND identifier = 10;
```

As a matter of interest, without the INDEX_JOIN hint, the optimizers will usually only join the single-column indexes.

MERGE(table)

Used to force the merging of a nested (inline) view with the main driving query. In the example given, the GROUP BY inline view is merged with the selection from the OWNERS table.

The hint can also be used for subqueries if the IN statement is uncorrelated; that is, it does not reference join columns in the main query.

```
SELECT /*+ MERGE(w) */ o.owner,
         w.num_wins, o.suburb
  FROM owners o,
      (SELECT owner, count(*) num_wins
        FROM winners
       WHERE position = 1
       GROUP BY owner) w
 WHERE o.owner    = w.owner
   AND w.num_wins > 15
 ORDER BY w.num_wins desc
```

MERGE_AJ

Provides substantial performance improvements by turning a nested loop operation for a NOT IN into a merge join operation (similar to HASH_AJ). This hint needs to be placed against the SELECT statement in the subquery, *not* in the main select clause.

```
SELECT count(*)
  FROM horses
 WHERE horse_name LIKE 'M%'
   AND horse_name NOT IN
 ( SELECT /*+ MERGE_AJ */ horse_name
     FROM horse_owners
    WHERE owner LIKE '%Lombardo%');
```

MERGE_SJ

This hint will often speed response times in an EXISTS subquery by returning the rows in the subquery only once.

```
SELECT count(*)
  FROM horses
 WHERE horse_name LIKE 'M%'
 AND EXISTS
 ( SELECT /*+ MERGE_SJ */ horse_name
    FROM horse_owners
   WHERE owner LIKE '%Lombardo%'
     AND horses.horse_name= horse_owners.horse_name)
```

There are some restrictions on this hint:

a. There must be only one table in the subquery.

b. The subquery can't be a subquery within a subquery.

c. The subquery must be correlated with an equality predicate.

d. The subquery must have no GROUP BY clause, CONNECT BY clause, or ROWNUM reference.

NL_AJ

Occasionally provides some performance improvements by forcing a nested loop operation for a NOT IN. However, nested loop performance is often inferior to that of the hash join and the sort merge join. The hint needs to be placed against the SELECT statement in the subquery, *not* in the main select clause.

```
SELECT count(*)
  FROM horses
 WHERE horse_name LIKE 'M%'
 AND horse_name NOT IN
 ( SELECT /*+ NL_AJ */ horse_name
    FROM horse_owners
   WHERE owner LIKE '%Lombardo%');
```

NL_SJ

This hint is similar to the HASH_SJ and MERGE_SJ hints, but uses the nested loop operation for the semi join.

```
SELECT count(*)
  FROM horses
 WHERE horse_name LIKE 'M%'
 AND EXISTS
```

```
( SELECT /*+ NL_SJ */ horse_name
   FROM horse_owners
  WHERE owner LIKE '%Lombardo%'
    AND horses.horse_name=
        horse_owners.horse_name)
```

There are some restrictions on this hint:

a. There must be only one table in the subquery.

b. It can't be a subquery within a subquery.

c. The subquery must be correlated with an equality predicate.

d. The subquery must have no GROUP BY, CONNECT BY, or ROWNUM reference.

NO_EXPAND

Prevents a query from being broken up into separate pieces, which is almost the reverse of the USE_CONCAT hint.

```
SELECT /*+ NO_EXPAND */ COUNT(*)
  FROM horse_owners
 WHERE identifier < 10 OR identifier > 20
```

NO_FACT(table)

Tells the cost-based optimizer that the table listed is *not* a fact table and should *not* be treated as such. This hint is used with STAR_TRANSFORMATION processing.

```
SELECT /*+ NO_FACT(results) */
```

NO_MERGE(table)

Prevents the merging of a nested (inline) view.

```
SELECT /*+ NO_MERGE(w) */ o.owner,
     w.num_wins, o.suburb
  FROM owners o,
    (SELECT owner, count(*) num_wins
     FROM winners
     WHERE position = 1
     GROUP BY owner) w
 WHERE o.owner    = w.owner
   AND w.num_wins > 15
 ORDER BY w.num_wins desc
```

NO_PUSH_PRED(table)

Prevents the join predicate from being pushed into an inline view.

```
SELECT /*+ NO_PUSH_PRED(v) */ count(*)
   FROM horses h,
      (SELECT w.horse_name, o.owner,
              w.position
         FROM winners w, owners o
        WHERE w.owner = o.owner) v
  WHERE h.horse_name = v.horse_name
    AND v.position = 1
```

NO_UNNEST

Prevents the merging of a subquery into the main statement body. Can only be used when UNNEST_SUBQUERY=TRUE.

```
SELECT /*+ NO_UNNEST */ count(*)
  FROM horses
 WHERE horse_name LIKE 'M%'
   AND horse_name NOT IN
 ( SELECT horse_name
     FROM horse_owners
    WHERE owner LIKE '%Lombardo%');
```

NOAPPEND

The opposite of APPEND; results in a conventional insert into a table. There is no guarantee that the data will be appended at the end of the table. The rows to be inserted do not bypass the buffer cache, and integrity constraints are respected.

```
INSERT /*+ NOAPPEND */ * INTO y
SELECT FROM winners;
```

NOCACHE(table)

Instructs the optimizer to position all blocks fetched for the specified table at the *least* recently used end of the LRU list in the buffer cache when performing a full table scan. This is the normal behavior for a full table scan.

```
SELECT /*+ FULL(winners) NOCACHE(winners)
       */ count(*)
   FROM winners
```

NOINDEX(table [index [index...]])

Eliminates the indexes listed from usage in the execution plan for a query.

```
SELECT /*+ NOINDEX(EMP EMP_NDX1) */
```

If a table is specified without an index, no indexes on the table can be used.

```
SELECT /*+ NOINDEX(EMP) */
```

NOPARALLEL(table)

Prevents Oracle from using parallelism (multiple processes) to scan the specified table. For example, assume you enable parallelism as follows:

```
ALTER TABLE x PARALLEL 2;
```

Oracle now attempts to use two processes in parallel whenever the table needs to be scanned. The following statement uses the NOPARALLEL hint to prevent that parallelism from occurring:

```
SELECT /*+ NOPARALLEL(x) */ COUNT(*)
FROM x;
```

NOPARALLEL_INDEX(table, index)

Ensures that parallel index processing does not occur for a partitioned index.

```
SELECT /*+ NOPARALLEL_INDEX(emp, emp_ndx) */
```

NOREWRITE

Prevents Oracle from utilizing materialized views based on a selected table. It is the exact reverse of the REWRITE hint.

```
SELECT /*+ NOREWRITE */ horse_name, owner, position,
COUNT(*)
  FROM results
GROUP BY horse_name, owner, position
```

ORDERED

Forces the optimizer to join tables in the same order as that in which they are specified in the FROM clause (left to right). This hint can give enormous performance gains in a reporting environment. It is also usually the case that the larger the number of tables in the FROM clause, the larger the benefits from this hint. Following is an example of its use:

```
SELECT /*+ ORDERED */
       acct_name, trans_date, amount,
       dept, address
  FROM trans t, account a, category c ,
       branch b, zip z
 WHERE t.trans_date > sysdate - 30
   AND a.zip        = z.zip
   AND z.state      = 'WA'
   AND t.account    between 700000 and
                    799999
   AND t.account    = a.account
   AND a.account    = 'ACTIVE'
   AND a.category   = c.category
   AND c.catgory    = 'RETAIL'
   AND t.branch_id  = b.branch_id
   AND b.branch     = 'BELLEVUE'
```

Usually the driving index, and thus the driving table, for a query are determined by the type of index, how many columns are in the index, the number of rows in the index, and so on. For example, a table that has a UNIQUE index column equality check in the WHERE clause will become a driving table over a table that has a NON-UNIQUE column specified in the WHERE clause.

Interestingly, if all things are equal, the cost-based optimizer will use the left to right order in the FROM clause, which is the exact reverse of the rule-based optimizer. However, in a complex query, it is rare to find all things equal in the WHERE clause. Use this hint to guarantee the join order.

ORDERED_PREDICATES

Causes WHERE clause predicates to be evaluated in the order in which they are listed in the WHERE clause. If you do not specify ORDERED_PREDICATES, Oracle will evaluate subqueries and user functions first.

> A USE: WHEN FTS ON LARGE TABLE AND CANNOT CREATE INDEX: USE THIS HINT AND PUT JOIN TO LARGE TABLE LAST.

```
SELECT ...
...
WHERE /*+ ORDERED_PREDICATES */
```

This is the only hint that goes in the WHERE clause
rather than after the keyword that begins the statement.

PARALLEL(table [,integer] [,integer])

Explicitly specifies the actual number of concurrent
query servers that will be used to service the query. The
first optional value specifies the degree of parallelism
(number of query servers) for the table. This is the number of processes assigned to perform the scan of the specified table in parallel on a single instance. The second
optional value specifies the number of Oracle parallel
server instances to split the query across. If you specify
PARALLEL(EMP, 4 2), there will be four parallel query
processes running on two separate parallel server
instances. If no parameters are specified, the default (calculated) degree of parallelism and number of parallel
servers is sourced from the parameters specified in the
INIT.ORA file.

The hint can be used for selects, updates, deletes, and
inserts. To get performance improvements using the parallel hint, your datafiles must be striped across multiple
disks. Don't set the degree of parallelism higher than the
number of disks that the table is striped over. Having
multiple processors will make the operation run even
faster, but only if the table is striped.

```
SELECT /*+ PARALLEL (x 4) */ COUNT(*)
FROM x;

SELECT /*+ PARALLEL (x 4 2) */ COUNT(*)
FROM x;

UPDATE /*+ PARALLEL (x 4) */ x
SET position = position+1;

DELETE /*+ parallel(x 4) */  from x;

INSERT INTO x
```

```
SELECT /*+ PARALLEL(winners 4) */ *
FROM winners;
```

PARALLEL_INDEX(table, index, degree of parallelism, cluster split)

Allows you to parallelize index range scans for partitioned indexes. Also allows the work to be done across multiple instances of a parallel server architecture. The following example tells the optimizer to utilize parallel index processing on the EMP table, which is partitioned, to use the EMP_NDX index, and to run at a parallel degree of four over two Oracle parallel server instances.

```
SELECT /*+ PARALLEL_INDEX(emp, emp_ndx, 4, 2) */
...
```

PQ_DISTRIBUTE(table [Outer Distribution] [Inner Distribution])

Used to improve parallel join performance. There are six possibilities for distribution hints, as listed in Table 6.

```
SELECT /*+ USE_HASH(o)
  PQ_DISTRIBUTE(o HASH, HASH) */ COUNT(*)
    FROM winners w, owners o
WHERE w.owner = o.owner;
```

Table 6. PQ_DISTRIBUTE combinations

Distribution combination	Meaning
HASH, HASH	Uses a hash function on the join keys for each query server process. Can be used for a hash join or sort merge join. Works best when tables are approximately the same size.
BROADCAST, NONE	Broadcasts all rows of the outer table to each of the parallel query servers. Use this when the outer table is considerably smaller than the inner table.
NONE, BROADCAST	Broadcasts all rows of the inner table to each of the parallel query servers. Use this option when the size of the inner table is much smaller than the outer table.
PARTITION, NONE	Maps the rows of the outer table using the partitioning of the inner table. The inner table must be partitioned and equi-joined on the join keys. This option works most effectively if the number of partitions in the outer table is equal to the number of parallel query processes utilized.

Table 6. PQ_DISTRIBUTE combinations (continued)

Distribution combination	Meaning
NONE, PARTITION	Maps the rows of the inner table using the partitioning of the outer table. The outer table must be partitioned on the join keys. Use this option when the number of partitions on the outer table is equal to the number of parallel query servers.
NONE, NONE	Causes each query server to perform a join operation between a pair of matching partitions, one from each table. Both tables must be equi-partitioned for this option to be used effectively.

PUSH_PRED(table)

Pushes the join predicate for a table into an inline view. Doing so can sometimes help the cost-based optimizer make better decisions.

```
SELECT /*+ PUSH_PRED(v) */ count(*)
    FROM horses h,
        (SELECT w.horse_name, o.owner,
                w.position
           FROM winners w, owners o
          WHERE w.owner = o.owner) v
   WHERE h.horse_name = v.horse_name
     AND v.position = 1
```

The difference in the execution plan for the example is that the HORSE_NAME in the WHERE clause is joined to the inline view as part of the inline view selection.

PUSH_SUBQ

Forces nonmerged subqueries to be evaluated as early as possible in the execution plan. Nonmerged subqueries are normally executed as the last step of an execution plan. This hint has no effect on a subquery if the subquery is over a remote table (as in a distributed SQL statement), or if the subquery uses a merge join.

```
SELECT count(*)
   FROM horses
  WHERE EXISTS
  ( SELECT /*+ PUSH_SUBQ */ 'x'
      FROM horse_owners
```

```
    WHERE owner LIKE '%Lombardo%'
      AND horses.horse_name=
          horse_owners.horse_name)
```

REWRITE

Allows Oracle to utilize materialized views based on a
selected table. In the example that follows, we have a
table that contains horse race results. We have created a
materialized view that stores the OWNER, HORSE_
NAME, POSITION, and the COUNT(*) for each of
those combinations.

```
CREATE MATERIALIZE VIEW LOG ON RESULTS
  WITH ROWID,
  PRIMARY KEY (HORSE_NAME, OWNER,
               RACE_DATE)
  INCLUDING NEW VALUES;

CREATE MATERIALIZED VIEW winning_horse_owners_vw
USING INDEX
REFRESH ON COMMIT
ENABLE QUERY REWRITE
AS SELECT horse_name, owner, position, COUNT(*)
    FROM results
    GROUP BY horse_name, owner, position;
```

In order for this materialized view to be useful, you must
have the INIT.ORA parameter QUERY_REWRITE_
ENABLED=TRUE, and the schema MUST HAVE the
privilege QUERY REWRITE assigned. For example:

```
GRANT QUERY REWRITE TO HROA;
```

The SQL query shown next is able to obtain all of the
data it requires from the view, and therefore the optimizer will use the view in preference to the table, despite
the SELECT being made against the table.

```
SELECT /*+ REWRITE */ horse_name, owner, position,
COUNT(*)
  FROM results
GROUP BY horse_name, owner, position;
```

ROWID(table)

Forces a table scan by ROWID for the specified table. The rowid is the physical disk address of the row.

```
SELECT /*+ ROWID(a) */ ename
     FROM emp a
     WHERE rowid > 'AAAGJ2AAIAAABn4AAA'
       AND surname like 'GURR%'
```

RULE

Uses the rule-based optimizer for the current statement block. You can achieve the same effect by having the CHOOSE option specified for the INIT.ORA parameter OPTIMIZER_MODE, and not analyzing the tables and indexes used in the SELECT statement.

STAR

Forces the largest table to be last in the join order. Typically the other tables should be lookup or reference tables. This hint is used extensively in data warehouse applications. STAR is only effective when you are joining at least three tables.

```
SELECT /*+ STAR */ h.horse_name, o.owner,
         r.position, r.location, r.race_date
    FROM results r, horses h, owners o
   WHERE h.horse_name like 'WI%'
     AND h.horse_name = r.horse_name
     AND r.owner      = o.owner;
```

STAR_TRANSFORMATION

Works on fact and dimension tables, and is similar to the STAR hint. The major difference is that it allows the cost-based optimizer to decide if it is worth transforming the statement into a new statement before determining the execution plan. By "transforming," I mean that the statement is broken into a number of subqueries that are able to take advantage of bitmap indexes.

To use this hint, it is essential that you have STAR_TRANSFORMATION_ENABLED=TRUE in your INIT. ORA file.

The most pronounced difference between this hint and the STAR hint is that the STAR_TRANSFORMATION will often combine bitmap indexes on the various fact table columns rather than using a Cartesian join. This is achieved by breaking the statement into subquery pieces.

```
SELECT /*+ STAR_TRANSFORMATION */
    ...
```

UNNEST

Merges the body of a subquery into the body of the main statement, which can often improve optimizer decision making. UNNEST can only be used when the session parameter UNNEST_SUBQUERY=TRUE.

```
SELECT /*+ UNNEST */ count(*)
    FROM horses
   WHERE horse_name LIKE 'M%'
     AND horse_name NOT IN
   ( SELECT horse_name
       FROM horse_owners
      WHERE owner LIKE '%Lombardo%');
```

USE_CONCAT

Forces the optimizer to take OR conditions in the WHERE clause and convert them to a UNION ALL query operation. In an example such as the one that follows, the index is scanned twice, once for each condition on the two sides of the OR. The data is then joined into one result set via a concatenation operation.

```
SELECT /*+ USE_CONCAT */ COUNT(*)
    FROM horse_owners
   WHERE identifier < 10 OR identifier > 20
```

USE_HASH (table)

A hash join is an alternative to a nested loop. A hash table is created in memory of the smallest table, and then the other table(s) is scanned, with its rows being compared to the hash. A hash join will run faster than a merge join (sort merge) if memory is adequate to hold the entire table that is being hashed. The entire join operation must be performed before a single row is returned

to the user. Therefore, hash joins are usually used for
reporting and batch processing.

```
SELECT /*+ USE_HASH(w o) */ count(*)
   FROM winners w, owners o
  WHERE w.owner like 'Mr M A Gurry'
    AND w.owner= o.owner
    AND o.suburb = 'RICHMOND'
```

A hash join can only be used for equality-based joins (=),
and not for range-based joins (<, <=, >, >=). A merge
join is often appropriate when a hash join cannot be
used.

NOTE

Don't confuse the HASH hint with USE_HASH.

USE_MERGE(table)

A merge join is an alternative to nested loop and hash
joins. All tables are sorted, unless all of the columns in
the WHERE clause are contained within an index. This
sort can be expensive and it explains why a hash join will
often run faster then a merge join.

```
SELECT /*+ USE_MERGE(w o) */ count(*)
   FROM winners w, owners o
  WHERE w.owner like 'Mr M A Gurry'
    AND w.owner < o.owner
    AND o.suburb = 'RICHMOND'
```

The entire set of data must be returned before a single
row is returned to the user. Therefore hash joins are usually used for reporting and batch processing.

NOTE

Don't confuse the MERGE hint and USE_MERGE.

Merge joins work effectively for equality-based joins as
well as for range-based joins. Merge joins also often run

much faster than a hash join when all of the columns in the WHERE clause are pre-sorted in an index.

USE_NL(table)

Forces the optimizer to join the specified table to another table (or subquery) using a nested loop join. The specified table is joined as the inner table of the nested loops. Nested loop joins are faster than sort/merge or hash joins at retrieving the first row of a query statement.

Online screens should definitely use nested loops, because data will be returned immediately. As a rule of thumb, if less than 10% of the rows are returned from the tables, consider using nested loops. Use hash joins or sort merges if 10% or more of the rows are being returned.

```
SELECT /*+ USE_NL(w o) */ count(*)
  FROM winners w, owners o
 WHERE w.owner like 'Mr M A Gurry'
   AND w.owner= o.owner
   AND o.suburb = 'RICHMOND'
```

Using DBMS_STATS to Manage Statistics

DBMS_STATS was introduced in Oracle8*i*; it provides critical functionality for the cost-based optimizer, including speeding the analyze process, allowing statistics to be modified, reverting back to previous statistics, and copying statistics from one schema (or database) to another.

Using DBMS_STATS to Analyze Faster

DBMS_STATS offers two powerful ways of speeding up the analyze process. First, you can analyze tables (not indexes) in parallel. Second, you can analyze only tables and their associated indexes that have had more than 10% of their rows modified through INSERT, UPDATE, or DELETE operations.

To analyze a schema's tables in parallel, use a command such as the following:

```
EXECUTE SYS.DBMS_STATS.GATHER_SCHEMA_STATS (OWNNAME=>
'HROA', ESTIMATE_PERCENT=>10, DEGREE=>4, CASCADE=>TRUE);
```

This command estimates statistics for the schema HROA. The DEGREE value specifies the degree of parallelism to use. CASCADE=>TRUE causes the indexes for each table to be analyzed as well. DBMS_STATS has a GATHER STALE option that will only analyze tables that have had more than 10% of their rows changed. To use it, you first need to turn on monitoring for your selected tables. For example:

```
ALTER TABLE WINNERS MONITORING;
```

You can observe information about the number of table changes for a given table by selecting from the USER_TAB_MODIFICATIONS view. You can see if monitoring is turned on for a particular table by selecting the MONITORING column from USER_TABLES.

With monitoring enabled, you can run the GATHER_SCHEMA_STATS package using the GATHER STALE option:

```
EXECUTE SYS.DBMS_STATS.GATHER_SCHEMA_STATS (OWNNAME=>
'HROA', ESTIMATE_PERCENT=>10, DEGREE=>4, CASCADE=>TRUE,
OPTIONS=>'GATHER STALE');
```

Because GATHER_STALE is specified, tables will only be analyzed if they have had 10% or more of their rows changed since the previous analyze.

Copying Statistics Using DBMS_STATS

DBMS_STATS gives you the ability to copy statistics from one schema to another, or from one database to another, using the following procedure:

Step 1. Create a table to store the statistics, if you have not already done so:

```
EXECUTE SYS.DBMS_STATS.CREATE_STATS_TABLE (OWNNAME=>
'HROA', STATTAB=>'HROA_STAT_TABLE');
```

Step 2. Populate the table with the statistics from the schema that you are copying from:

```
EXECUTE SYS.DBMS_STATS.EXPORT_SCHEMA_STATS (OWNNAME=>
'HROA', STATTAB=>'HROA_STAT_TABLE', STATID=>
'HROA_21SEP_2001');
```

Step 3. If you are copying statistics to a different database, such as from production to development, export and import that statistics table as required:

```
exp hroa/secret@prod file=stats tables=hroa_stat_table
```

```
imp hroa/secret@dev file=stats tables=hroa_stat_table
```

Step 4. Populate the statistics in the target schema's dictionary. In the following example, statistics are being loaded for the schema HROA_TEST from the table named HROA_STAT_TABLE:

```
EXECUTE SYS.DBMS_STATS.IMPORT_SCHEMA_STATS (OWNNAME=>
'HROA_TEST', STATTAB=>'HROA_STAT_TABLE', STATID=>
'HROA_21SEP_2001', STATOWN=> 'HROA');
```

Manipulating Statistics Using DBMS_STATS

Often you will want to determine if the cost-based optimizer will use the same execution plan in production as it is using in the current development and test databases. You can achieve this by using DBMS_STATS.SET_TABLE_STATS to modify the statistics for a table in your development or for a test database to match those in your production database. The optimizer uses the number of rows, number of blocks, and number of distinct values for a column to determine whether an index or a full table scan should be used.

The following example assumes that your production WIN-NERS table is going to have 1,000,000 rows in 6,000 blocks:

```
EXECUTE SYS.DBMS_STATS.SET_TABLE_STATS (OWNNAME=>
'HROA_DEV', TABNAME=>'WINNERS', NUMROWS=> 1000000,
NUMBLKS=> 6000);
```

Regardless of how many rows you really have in your test database, the cost-based optimizer will now behave as if there were 1,000,000.

The optimizer also uses the number of distinct values for each column to decide on index usage. If the number of distinct values is less than 10% of the number of rows in the table, the optimizer will usually decide to perform a full table scan in preference to using an index on the table column. Change the percentage of distinct values for a column as follows:

```
EXECUTE SYS.DBMS_STATS.SET_COLUMN_STATS (OWNNAME=>
'F70PSOFT', TABNAME=>'PS_LED_AUTH_TBL',
COLNAME=>'OPRID', DISTCNT=>971);
```

Reverting to Previous Statistics

Usually, re-analyzing a schema and specifying a high percent-age of rows for the sample size will improve performance. Unfortunately, the occasional hiccup will occur when you re-analyze tables. Sometimes the new statistics produce much worse execution plans than before. You can avoid the risk of a major screw up by using the DBMS_STATS package to save a copy of your current statistics just in case you need to restore them later. This requires the following steps:

Step 1. Export your schema statistics to your statistics table. If you don't already have a statistics table, you can create it using the DBMS_STATS.CREATE_STATS_TABLE proce-dure. The export is performed as follows:

```
EXECUTE SYS.DBMS_STATS.EXPORT_SCHEMA_STATS (OWNNAME=>
'HROA', STATTAB=>'HROA_STAT_TABLE', STATID=>
'PRE_21SEP_2001');
```

Step 2. Gather your new statistics:

```
EXECUTE SYS.DBMS_STATS.GATHER_SCHEMA_STATS (OWNNAME=>
'HROA', ESTIMATE_PERCENT=>10, DEGREE=>4, CASCADE=>TRUE);
```

Step 3. If there are problems with unsuitable execution paths being selected as a result of the new statistics, revert back to the previous statistics by loading the previous statistics from the statistics table:

```
EXECUTE SYS.DBMS_STATS.IMPORT_SCHEMA_STATS (OWNNAME=>
'HROA', STATTAB=>'HROA_STAT_TABLE', STATID=>
'PRE_21SEP_2001');
```

Using Outlines for Consistent Execution Plans

Oracle introduced outlines in Oracle8*i* to allow you to have a pre-defined execution plan for a SQL statement. Consistency can then be provided without changing the actual SQL. Outlines can be used for packaged software to provide execution plan stability without the need to change the application's SQL.

Recording Outlines

An outline is nothing more than a stored execution plan that Oracle uses rather than computing a new plan based on current table statistics. Before you can use outlines, you must record some. You can record outlines for a single statement, for all statements issued by a single session, or for all statements issued to an instance.

Recording an outline for a SQL statement

You can record the outlines for a particular statement using the CREATE OR REPLACE OUTLINE command as follows:

```
CREATE OR REPLACE OUTLINE aug0901
FOR CATEGORY harness_racing
ON select *
```

```
        from winners
    where owner > 'G%';
```

In this example, aug0901 is the name of the specific outline being created, and harness_racing is the name of a category, or group, or related outlines.

Recording outlines for all of a session's SQL

You can turn on the recording of outlines for a session by using the ALTER SESSION CREATE_STORED_OUT-LINES command.

Specify a category name to save outlines into a specific category:

```
ALTER SESSION
SET CREATE_STORED_OUTLINES
    =GENERAL_LEDGER;
```

Specify TRUE to record outlines in the default category, which is named DEFAULT:

```
ALTER SESSION
  SET CREATE_STORED_OUTLINES=TRUE;
```

Specify FALSE to disable the recording of stored outlines:

```
ALTER SESSION
  SET CREATE_STORED_OUTLINES=FALSE;
```

Recording outlines for the whole system

The syntax to turn on recording of outlines system-wide is very similar to the ALTER SESSION syntax. Simply use ALTER SYSTEM instead of ALTER SESSION. For example:

```
ALTER SYSTEM
  SET CREATE_STORED_OUTLINES
      =GENERAL_LEDGER NOOVERRIDE;
```

The NOOVERRIDE option will avoid the complete deletion of the GENERAL_LEDGER outlines in the example shown. If NOOVERRIDE had not been specified, all statements stored in the GENERAL_LEDGER category would have been removed. When NOOVERRIDE is specified, new statements have their outlines added to the existing category. If the same statement appears with an updated outline, the new outline will be stored.

Likewise, to turn off outline recording system-wide:

```
ALTER SYSTEM
   SET CREATE_STORED_OUTLINES=FALSE;
```

Enabling Outlines

You now have your outlines stored away. In order for Oracle to use them, you must enable them.

Enabling outlines for a session

You can enable the usage of outlines for a session by setting the ALTER SESSION USE_STORED_OUTLINES command.

Specify a category name to use the outlines in that category:

```
ALTER SESSION
   SET USE_STORED_OUTLINES
      =GENERAL_LEDGER;
```

Specify TRUE to use outlines from the DEFAULT category:

```
ALTER SESSION
   SET USE_STORED_OUTLINES= TRUE;
```

Specify FALSE to disable (turn off) the use of outlines:

```
ALTER SESSION
   SET USE_STORED_OUTLINES= FALSE;
```

Enabling outlines for the whole system

To enable outlines system-wide, use ALTER SYSTEM instead of ALTER SESSION. Otherwise, the syntax is the same. For example:

```
ALTER SYSTEM
   SET USE_STORED_OUTLINES
   =GENERAL_LEDGER NOOVERRIDE;
```

In this case, all existing OUTLINES can continue to be used with the GENERAL_LEDGER outlines that are now used as well. If NOOVERRIDE was not specified, the GENERAL_LEDGER outlines will replace those currently being used.

Likewise, to disable outlines system-wide:

```
ALTER SYSTEM
    SET USE_STORED_OUTLINES= FALSE;
```

Managing Outlines

You can view outlines to verify that they have been recording correctly and to see what execution plan has been recorded. You can also transfer outlines from one schema to another.

Viewing your outlines

To view outlines in order to test whether they are recording, select from the OUTLN.OL$ and OUTLN.OL$HINTS tables. OUTLN.OL$ contains the SQL statements, and OUTLN.OL$HINTS contains the optimizer hints to use with the statements.

In addition to the tables owned by the OUTLN user, you can also view your own personal outlines by querying the USER_OUTLINES and USER_OUTLINE_HINTS views (also see the DBA_ and ALL_ views). For example:

```
SELECT    uo.name, sql_text , hint
   FROM user_outlines uo,
        user_outline_hints uoh
  WHERE    uo.name = uoh.name
  ORDER BY join_pos

SYS_OUTLINE_010805222913599
select owner ||','|| first ||','|| second ||',' ||third
||','
 ||points
 from winners_current_month
where points > 4
and owner is not null
```

```
order by points desc
NO_FACT(WINNERS_CURRENT_MONTH)
```

To observe if an outline is currently being used for SQL statements, you can look in the OUTLINE_CATEGORY column
of the V$SQL table for the row containing the SQL state-
ment you are interested in.

Transferring outlines between databases

Transferring outlines across databases is simply a case of
export and import. For example:

```
EXP OUTLN/OUTLN FILE=OUTLN_21SEP2001.DMP TABLES=OL$,
OL$HINTS BUFFER=262144

IMP OUTLN/OUTLN FILE=OUTLN_21SEP2001.DMP BUFFER=262144
IGNORE=Y
```

This example transfers outlines for all schemas. After the
import, you can delete rows from the OL$ and OL$HINTS
tables in the target database for schemas that you don't wish
to transfer.

Dealing with literals

Many applications use literals instead of bind variables. This
means that SQL statements will often be similar, and should
use the same execution plan. However, since there is one
value, the literal value, different from one statement to the
next, that sharing of execution plans does not happen.

Unfortunately, Oracle does not assist us here, even with
CURSOR_SHARING = FORCE or SIMILAR. Cursor sharing does not work for outlines. I am sure that Oracle will
address this issue in the future.